MW01038251

THE BAKER
FUNERAL
HANDBOOK

Also by Paul E. Engle

The Baker Wedding Handbook

Baker's Worship Handbook: Traditional and Contemporary Service Resources

Discovering the Fullness of Worship

God's Answers for Life's Needs

The Governor Drove Us Up the Wall: A Guide to Nehemiah

Guarding and Growing: A Study in 2 Peter

Worship Planbook: A Manual for Worship Leaders

THE BAKER
FUNERAL
HANDBOOK

Paul E. Engle, editor

BakerBooks

a division of Baker Publishing Group
Grand Rapids, Michigan

© 1996, 2017 by Paul E. Engle

Published by Baker Books
a division of Baker Publishing Group
P.O. Box 6287, Grand Rapids, MI 49516-6287
www.bakerbooks.com

Printed in the United States of America

An updated edition of *Baker's Funeral Handbook*

Library of Congress Cataloging-in-Publication Data is on file at the Library of Congress, Washington, DC.

ISBN 978-0-8010-1968-5

Unless otherwise indicated, Scripture quotations are from the Holy Bible, New International Version®. NIV®. Copyright © 1973, 1978, 1984, 2011 by Biblica, Inc.™ Used by permission of Zondervan. All rights reserved worldwide. www.zondervan.com

Scripture quotations labeled ASV are from the American Standard Version of the Bible.

Scripture quotations labeled HCSB are from the Holman Christian Standard Bible®, copyright © 1999, 2000, 2002, 2003, 2009 by Holman Bible Publishers. Used by permission. Holman Christian Standard Bible®, Holman CSB®, and HCSB® are federally registered trademarks of Holman Bible Publishers.

Scripture quotations labeled KJV are from the King James Version of the Bible.

Scripture quotations labeled NRSV are from the New Revised Standard Version of the Bible, copyright © 1989, by the Division of Christian Education of the National Council of the Churches of Christ in the United States of America. Used by permission. All rights reserved.

Scripture quotations labeled RSV are from the Revised Standard Version of the Bible, copyright 1952 [2nd edition, 1971] by the Division of Christian Education of the National Council of the Churches of Christ in the United States of America. Used by permission. All rights reserved.

17   18   19   20   21   22   23   7   6   5   4   3   2   1

To: John, Matthew, Katie, Andrew, Carson

"We will tell the next generation the praiseworthy deeds
of the LORD, his power, and the wonders he has done."

Psalm 78:4

Contents

Contents

Appendixes

Preface

I now feel so weaned from earth, my affections so much in Heaven, that I can leave you all without regret, yet I do not love you less, but God more.

William Wilberforce

Labor now to live so, that at the hour of death thou mayest rather rejoice than fear. . . . Happy is he that always hath the hour of his death before his eyes, and daily prepareth himself to die. . . . Be thou therefore always in a readiness, and so lead thy life that death may never take thee unprepared.

Thomas à Kempis

In the face of death, grieving church members and their families need the comforting presence of a pastor as much as, if not more than, at any other time. Pastors are often called upon to minister to the dying in homes and in hospitals. Immediately following a death, pastors are expected to meet with the surviving family to comfort as well as to counsel concerning the funeral or memorial service and burial arrangements. Pastors then preside over these services as representatives of Christ's church.

Why Have Funerals and Memorial Services?

Funerals and memorial services provide an opportunity for family and friends to honor and remember the departed one. Such services provide a means for the Christian community to show support and sympathy for those who grieve. This is an occasion to affirm one's faith in the resurrected Christ and the eternal home he is preparing for those who know him as Savior and Lord. At the graveside committal service the body or ashes of the deceased are respectfully laid to rest in anticipation of the future resurrection.

Where Can Pastors Turn for Direction in Planning Funerals and Memorial Services?

Full funeral liturgies cannot be found in the pages of Scripture. We are therefore given freedom to employ scriptural truths to develop appropriate Christian funerals (with a casket or cremated remains present) and memorial services (without a casket and sometimes following cremation). Whereas in past years pastors commonly turned to their own traditional denominational services for the full spectrum of funeral needs, we have witnessed a gradual shift away from this standardized approach. Many pastors, taking into account the circumstances of the death as well as the unique background of the deceased, are recognizing the need to be aware of the funeral customs of a wider diversity of denominations. Denominational distinctions are breaking down as funeral and memorial services today often vary greatly. Personalized services with more congregational participation have become more frequent.

The Baker Funeral Handbook provides pastors from multiple denominations with comprehensive resources to tailor creative funerals, memorial services, and committal services. A quick scan through the table of contents will reveal the wide range of resources, especially helpful when one is called upon to preside over a service with a minimum of preparation time.

How Can This Handbook Be Used?

Here are some examples of ways this book might prove helpful:

- Experienced pastors can profit from the stimulation of being exposed to funeral and memorial service customs from a variety of denominations. Rather than purchasing eleven different denominational handbooks, pastors can use this single volume to construct a creative and personalized service.
- Pastors who face special needs such as conducting a funeral for one who committed suicide, a request for a memorial service for a stillborn infant, the funeral for a child, the death of someone in an accident, or a funeral for someone who does not profess

to be a Christian, can find in these pages helpful, specific, and appropriate suggestions.

- Ministers who need to put together a funeral message within a short space of time will find resources in the form of suggested texts, illustrations, quotations, last words of noted individuals, and guidelines for such messages.

- When visiting with the dying, pastors will find in these pages appropriate Scripture texts and ideas for prayer, such as suggestions on how to pray with someone dying of AIDS or someone suffering from Alzheimer's disease.

- The charts in the appendixes may be photocopied for use in planning funeral and memorial services, for working with parishioners to preplan funeral preferences, or for keeping a record of services performed.

- Pastors may wish to recommend this book to parishioners who request help in preplanning funeral or memorial services for themselves or family members.

- Ministerial students or new pastors who face their first funerals, memorial services, or committal services and need direction will find it here.

- Seminary or Bible college instructors may find this a useful manual to recommend to their students or to use in pastoral duties classes.

Conducting funerals and memorial services is one of the highest privileges for ministers of the gospel of the resurrected Christ. This handbook is offered with the prayer that you will find in its pages valuable tools that will enable you to minister effectively to the dying and their families. May the carrying out of our solemn, sacred duties only serve to heighten our anticipation of the new heaven and new earth where it is promised, "He will wipe every tear from their eyes. There will be no more death or mourning or crying or pain, for the old order of things has passed away" (Rev. 21:4).

Having served faithfully in ministering to the dying and their families, may we echo the words of Matthew Henry (1662–1714), who concluded his own life with this reflection: "A life spent in the service of God and communion with Him, is the most comfortable and pleasant life that one can live in this present world."

PART I

Denominational Funeral and Memorial Services

1

Baptist

Opening Words

But as it is written:

> What eye did not see and ear did not hear,
> and what never entered the human mind—
> God prepared this for those who love Him.
> Now God has revealed these things to us by the Spirit, for
>   the Spirit searches everything, even the depths of God.
>   (1 Cor. 2:9–10 HCSB)

> Lord, happy is the man You discipline
> and teach from Your law
> to give him relief from troubled times
> until a pit is dug for the wicked.
> The Lord will not forsake His people
> or abandon His heritage. (Ps. 94:12–14 HCSB)

See how happy the man is God corrects;
so do not reject the discipline of the Almighty. (Job 5:17
    HCSB)

Because you have made the Lord—my refuge,
the Most High—your dwelling place,
no harm will come to you;
no plague will come near your tent.
For He will give His angels orders concerning you,
to protect you in all your ways.
They will support you with their hands
so that you will not strike your foot against a stone.
You will tread on the lion and the cobra;
you will trample the young lion and the serpent.

Because he is lovingly devoted to Me,
I will deliver him;
I will protect him because he knows My name.
When he calls out to Me, I will answer him;
I will be with him in trouble.
I will rescue him and give him honor. (Ps. 91:9–15 HCSB)

Hymn

A hymn may be sung or read, or suitable poetry may be used instead.

Scripture

Select one or more of the following Scripture passages.

Beloved, let us seek comfort in the assurances of God's Word.

If we would be assured of God's care for us, we need the following words:

> The LORD is my shepherd;
> there is nothing I lack.
> He lets me lie down in green pastures;
> He leads me beside quiet waters.
> He renews my life;
> He leads me along the right paths
> for His name's sake.
> Even when I go through the darkest valley,
> I fear no danger,
> for You are with me;
> Your rod and Your staff—they comfort me.
>
> You prepare a table before me
> in the presence of my enemies;
> You anoint my head with oil;
> my cup overflows.
> Only goodness and faithful love will pursue me
> all the days of my life,
> and I will dwell in the house of the LORD
> as long as I live. (Ps. 23 HCSB)

We know that all things work together for the good of those who love God: those who are called according to His purpose. For those He foreknew He also predestined to be conformed to the image of His Son, so that He would be the firstborn among many brothers. And those He predestined, He also called; and those He called, He also justified; and those He justified, He also glorified.

What then are we to say about these things?
If God is for us, who is against us?
He did not even spare His own Son
but offered Him up for us all;
how will He not also with Him grant us everything?
Who can bring an accusation against God's elect?
God is the One who justifies.
Who is the one who condemns?
Christ Jesus is the One who died,
but even more, has been raised;
He also is at the right hand of God
and intercedes for us.
Who can separate us from the love of Christ?
Can affliction or anguish or persecution
or famine or nakedness or danger or sword?
As it is written:
Because of You
we are being put to death all day long;
we are counted as sheep to be slaughtered.
No, in all these things we are more than victorious
through Him who loved us.
For I am persuaded that not even death or life,
angels or rulers,
things present or things to come, hostile powers,
height or depth, or any other created thing
will have the power to separate us

from the love of God that is in Christ Jesus our Lord! (Rom.
8:28–39 HCSB)

Then one of the elders asked me, "Who are these people robed in white, and where did they come from?"

I said to him, "Sir, you know."

Then he told me:

> These are the ones coming out of the great tribulation.
> They washed their robes and made them white
> in the blood of the Lamb.
> For this reason they are before the throne of God,
> and they serve Him day and night in His sanctuary.
> The One seated on the throne will shelter them:
> They will no longer hunger;
> they will no longer thirst;
> the sun will no longer strike them,
> nor will any heat.
> For the Lamb who is at the center of the throne
> will shepherd them;
> He will guide them to springs of living waters,
> and God will wipe away every tear from their eyes. (Rev.
> 7:13–17 HCSB)

If we would be assured of an eternal home, let our hearts be consoled by these words:

> Your heart must not be troubled. Believe in God; believe also in Me.
> In My Father's house are many dwelling places; if not, I would have
> told you. I am going away to prepare a place for you. If I go away and

prepare a place for you, I will come back and receive you to Myself, so that where I am you may be also. (John 14:1–3 HCSB)

We do not want you to be uninformed, brothers, concerning those who are asleep, so that you will not grieve like the rest, who have no hope. Since we believe that Jesus died and rose again, in the same way God will bring with Him those who have fallen asleep through Jesus. For we say this to you by a revelation from the Lord: We who are still alive at the Lord's coming will certainly have no advantage over those who have fallen asleep. For the Lord Himself will descend from heaven with a shout, with the archangel's voice, and with the trumpet of God, and the dead in Christ will rise first. Then we who are still alive will be caught up together with them in the clouds to meet the Lord in the air and so we will always be with the Lord. Therefore encourage one another with these words. (1 Thess. 4:13–18 HCSB)

Prayer

Having heard God speaking to us in his Word, let us now take our sorrow to him, being assured that he will hear us by the following blessed words:

Draw near to God, and He will draw near to you. Cleanse your hands, sinners, and purify your hearts, double-minded people! . . . Humble yourselves before the Lord, and He will exalt you. (James 4:8, 10 HCSB)

Let us pray . . .

Hymn

A hymn may be sung or read, or suitable poetry may be used instead.

Address

If deemed advisable.

Hymn

A hymn may be sung or read, or suitable poetry may be used instead.

Closing Words

The services here are now concluded, and we will proceed to the cemetery where the interment will take place.

Minister takes his place in the lead of the pallbearers and walks from home or church in this order to the funeral vehicles. Upon arrival at the cemetery, the minister again takes his place in the lead of the pallbearers and walks in this order to the grave.

Procession to the Grave

The minister may say the following, as he walks in the lead of the procession.

Then I heard a voice from heaven saying, "Write: The dead who die in the Lord from now on are blessed."

"Yes," says the Spirit, "let them rest from their labors, for their works follow them!" (Rev. 14:13 HCSB)

> You guide me with Your counsel,
> and afterward You will take me up in glory.
> Who do I have in heaven but You?
> And I desire nothing on earth but You.
> My flesh and my heart may fail,
> but God is the strength of my heart,
> my portion forever. (Ps. 73:24–26 HCSB)

Lowering of the Casket

When the casket has been placed on the supports ready for lowering into the grave, the minister takes his stand at the head of the grave. Then he may say as the casket is lowered:

Brothers, I tell you this: Flesh and blood cannot inherit the kingdom of God, and corruption cannot inherit incorruption. Listen! I am telling you a mystery:

> We will not all fall asleep,
> but we will all be changed,
> in a moment, in the blink of an eye,
> at the last trumpet.
> For the trumpet will sound,
> and the dead will be raised incorruptible,

and we will be changed.
For this corruptible must be clothed
with incorruptibility,
and this mortal must be clothed
with immortality.
When this corruptible is clothed
with incorruptibility,
and this mortal is clothed
with immortality,
then the saying that is written will take place:
Death has been swallowed up in victory.
Death, where is your victory?
Death, where is your sting?
Now the sting of death is sin,
and the power of sin is the law.
But thanks be to God, who gives us the victory
through our Lord Jesus Christ!

Therefore, my dear brothers, be steadfast, immovable, always excelling in the Lord's work, knowing that your labor in the Lord is not in vain. (1 Cor. 15:50–58 HCSB)

Words of Committal

My Friends: Whereas, death hath once more invaded our ranks and removed from the walk of life our beloved brother/sister _____, his/her soul having departed to dwell in "the undiscovered country from whose bourn no traveler returns,"* it has become our sad duty to commit his/her body to the grave—earth to earth, ashes to ashes, dust to dust—and our inspiring privilege to commend his/her soul to our Maker, Father, and Redeemer, in the confident hope of the coming again of our Lord and Savior Jesus Christ, the resurrection of the body from the grave, and the joyous life reserved for the children of light in the realms of glory.

Then the grave may be filled or canopied and decorated with flowers, after which the people may be dismissed by prayer or benediction.

Benediction

"And the peace of God, which surpasses every thought, will guard your hearts and minds in Christ Jesus. . . . Now to our God and Father be glory forever and ever. Amen" (Phil. 4:7, 20 HCSB).

James Randolph Hobbs, *The Pastor's Manual* (Nashville: Broadman & Holman, 1962), 21–30. Renewal, 1990, The Sunday School Board of the Southern Baptist Convention. All rights reserved. Used by permission. Adapted with quotations from the King James Version replaced by the Holman Christian Standard Bible, 2009.

---

*William Shakespeare, *Hamlet*, act 3, scene 1. *Bourn* means small stream.

2

Christian Church

Opening Prayer

Scripture Reading

> Jesus said to her, "I am the resurrection and the life. The one who believes in me will live, even though they die; and whoever lives by believing in me will never die. Do you believe this?" (John 11:25–26)

Brothers and sisters, we do not want you to be uninformed about those who sleep in death, so that you do not grieve like the rest of mankind, who have no hope. For we believe that Jesus died and rose again, and so we believe that God will bring with Jesus those who have fallen asleep in him. According to the Lord's word, we tell you that we who are still alive, who are left until the coming of the Lord, will certainly not precede those who have fallen asleep. For the Lord himself will come down from heaven, with a loud command, with the voice of the archangel and with the trumpet call of God, and the dead in Christ will rise first. After that, we who are still alive and are left will be caught up together with them in the clouds to meet the Lord in the air. And so we will be with the Lord forever. Therefore encourage each other with these words. (1 Thess. 4:13–18)

Introduction

God offers us these encouraging words: One day, Jesus "will wipe every tear from [your] eyes. There will be no more death or mourning or crying or pain, for the old order of things has passed away" (Rev. 21:4). There are a lot of things that are hard about today. The hardest part about a day like today is that death really means separation. And today, _____'s family is separated from her/him.

_____ loved family. Her/his favorite times were with her/his family (children, grandchildren, and great-grandchildren). They were the absolute joy of her/his life.

_____ enjoyed life. (*Tell of some of the deceased person's activities.*) And death means a separation from those days, those times, and her/him.

But the Bible tells us that one day there will be a place where that kind of separation does not exist.

I. There will be no more death.

The one thing that sets Christianity apart from every other world religion is that it is the only faith with a founder who conquered death!

30

All others died and stayed dead. Jesus died and came back to life! If there is a part of you that looks at this death and says, "It's not right; it's just not right," you are correct. It's not right! And Jesus came to make it right. And you can trust someone who conquered death to make it right. That's why his Word says, "There will be no more death." One day there will be no more separation!

Consequently the Bible also promises that one day

II. There will be no more mourning.

There are a lot of things we feel right now:

Fortunate to have known _____

Personal remembrances will be shared here—add your own.

III. There will be no more pain.

There is comfort in that. Like all of us, parts of _____'s life were painful.

Tell of times of struggle.

So how do we make it in times like these?

First Thessalonians 4:18 says, "Encourage each other with these words." What "words"?

The words we've spoken today. And the words of God. One day, Jesus "will wipe every tear from [your] eyes. There will be no more death or mourning or crying or pain, for the old order of things has passed away" (Rev. 21:4).

Closing Prayer

Service by Dave Ferguson, in Guthrie Veech, *Christian Minister's Manual, Updated and Expanded* (Cincinnati: Standard Publishing, 2012), 161–63. Used by permission.

3

Christian Reformed Church

Prelude

The Placing of the Pall (optional)

When the pall is placed in the presence of the congregation, one of the following may be said in addition to or in place of the opening sentences.

Leader: "For all of you who were baptized into Christ have clothed yourselves with Christ" (Gal. 3:27). In his/her baptism, _____ put on Christ; in the day of Christ's coming, he/she shall be clothed with Christ's glory.

   Or

Leader: "All of us who were baptized into Christ Jesus were baptized into his death. We were therefore buried with him through baptism into death in order that, just as Christ was raised from the dead through the glory of the Father, we too may live a new life. For if we have been united with him in a death like his, we will certainly also be united with him in a resurrection like his" (Rom. 6:3–5).

> *People:* **Those who believe in him, though they die, yet shall they live.**

A pall is placed over the coffin.

Procession

Opening Sentences

One or several of the following sentences may be used.

Leader: The psalmist proclaims: "My heart is glad and my tongue rejoices; my body also will rest secure, because you will not abandon me to the realm of the dead, nor will you let your faithful one see decay."

> *People:* **"You have made known to me the path of life; you will fill me with joy in your presence, with eternal pleasures at your right hand" (Ps. 16:9–11).**

Or

Leader: "God is our refuge and strength, an ever-present help in trouble."

> *People:* **"Therefore we will not fear" (Ps. 46:1–2).**

Or

Leader: "Our help is in the name of the LORD, the Maker of heaven and earth."

> *People:* **Amen (Ps. 124:8).**

Or

Leader: Jesus says: "I am the resurrection and the life. The one who believes in me will live, even though they die; and whoever lives by believing in me will never die. Do you believe this?"

> *People:* **"Yes, Lord, [we] believe that you are the Messiah, the Son of God, who is to come into the world" (John 11:25–27).**

Or

Leader: The apostle Paul writes: "All of us who were baptized into Christ Jesus were baptized into his death. We were therefore buried with him through baptism into death in order that, just as Christ was raised from the dead through the glory of the Father, we too may live a new life."

> *People:* **"For if we have been united with him in a death like his, we will certainly also be united with him in a resurrection like his" (Rom. 6:3–5).**

Or

Leader: "If we live, we live to the Lord; and if we die, we die to the Lord."

> *People*: **"So, whether we live or die, we belong to the Lord" (Rom. 14:8).**

Or

Leader: "We believe that Jesus died and rose again, and so we believe that God will bring with Jesus those who have fallen asleep in him."

> *People*: **"And so we will be with the Lord forever" (1 Thess. 4:14, 17).**

Or

Leader: What is your only comfort in life and in death?

> *People*: **That I am not my own, but belong, body and soul, in life and in death, to my faithful Savior Jesus Christ (*Heidelberg Catechism* Q & A 1).**

Psalm, Hymn, or Spiritual Song

Congregation stands.

Call to Prayer

Select one of the following to call the people to prayer.

Brothers and sisters, let us now turn our hearts to God in prayer that he might strengthen our faith, and grant us his peace and comfort.

Or

We have gathered here in sorrow and in hope at the death of _____. Let us now share our grief with God and seek his comfort.

Opening Prayer(s)

One or more of the following prayers may be offered, either in responsive form or by the officiant.

Leader: Eternal God and Father, gathered around your throne in glory is that great company of all those who have kept the faith, finished their race, and now rest from their labors.

> *People:* **We give you praise and thanks that you have now received _____ into your presence.**

Leader: Help us here on earth to believe that which we cannot see, trusting in Christ who said, "I go to prepare a place for you."

> *People:* **Bring us all at last with all your saints into the joy of your eternal home, through Jesus Christ our Lord. Amen.**

Or

Leader: Eternal God, shepherd of your people, on this solemn occasion we feel the fleeting passage of life; and we know how fragile is our existence on this tiny planet amid the spinning galaxies. We confess with the prophet:

> *People:* **All flesh is grass, and all its glory is like the flowers of the field. The grass withers and the flowers fall . . .**

Leader: Yet we also confess:

> *People:* **The word of our God stands forever.**

Leader: Teach us to number our days that we may gain a heart of wisdom. We look to you as frightened children look to their mother, for you alone can comfort us.

> *People:* **Have mercy on us, O God. See our hearts and hear our cries, and lead us all, as pilgrims, through this valley of death's shadow into the light of the resurrection of Jesus Christ your Son, our Lord. Amen.**

Or

Leader: God of grace and glory, we remember before you this day our brother/sister _____. We thank you for giving him/her to us, his/her family and friends, to know and to love as a companion on this earthly pilgrimage. In your boundless compassion, console us who mourn. Give us faith to see in death the gateway of eternal life, so that in quiet confidence we may continue our course on earth, until by your call, we are united with those who have gone before, through Jesus Christ our Lord.

> *People:* **Amen.**

Or

Leader: Most merciful God, whose wisdom is beyond our understanding: deal graciously with _____'s family and friends in their grief. Surround them with your love, that they may not be overwhelmed by their loss, but have confidence in your goodness and strength to meet the days to come, through Jesus Christ our Lord.

> *People:* **Amen.**

At the death of a child.

Leader: Loving Father, you are nearest to us when we need you most. In this hour of sorrow we turn to you, knowing that you love us and trusting in your perfect wisdom. We thank you for the gift of this child and for his/her baptism into your church, for the joy he/she gave all who knew him/her, for the precious memories that will always abide with us, and especially for the assurance that he/she lives forever in the joy and peace of your presence, through Jesus Christ our Lord.

> *People:* **Amen.**

Remembrance

A family member(s) or friend(s) may offer a remembrance of the life and gifts of the deceased.

Prayer for Illumination

A prayer for illumination may be said by the officiant or in unison by the congregation before the Scriptures are read. Or the congregation may sing a prayer song, such as "O Word of God Incarnate."

Lord Jesus Christ, you are the living Word of God. To whom else should we go? For you have the words of eternal life. As we listen to your Word, may your Spirit write its message on our hearts and feed our souls with its nourishing truth. Amen.

The Readings

It is suggested that the Scriptures be read in this order: Old Testament, Psalm, New Testament, and Gospel. Usually no more than one passage should be read from each category. If one of the passages to be read will be the basis for the sermon, it should be read last, with an intervening psalm or hymn between it and the other passages read. The interval might also be an appropriate time for the remembrance.

Old Testament

Psalm (read, recited, or sung)

Epistle

Gospel

[Hymn, psalm, or remembrance]

Sermon lesson

Sermon

The brief sermon should proclaim the gospel and offer hope and comfort to the bereaved. Especially if there was no remembrance, memories of the life of the deceased and expressions of gratitude to God for his/her life ought to be included.

Psalm, Hymn, or Scriptural Song and/or Creed or Other Statement of Faith

A creed or other statement of faith is also suggested in the committal service. If the Apostles' Creed is used for the funeral service, select a different statement of faith for the committal.

All: I believe in God, the Father almighty, creator of heaven and earth. I believe in Jesus Christ, his only Son, our Lord, who was conceived by the Holy Spirit and born of the Virgin Mary. He suffered under Pontius Pilate, was crucified, died, and was buried; he descended to hell. On the third day he rose again from the dead. He ascended to heaven, and is seated at the right hand of God the Father almighty. From there he will come again to judge the living and the dead. I believe in the Holy Spirit, the holy catholic Church, the communion of saints, the forgiveness of sins, the resurrection of the body, and the life everlasting. Amen.

Prayers

One or more of the following prayers may be offered.

Leader: Let us pray to our loving God through Jesus Christ his Son, who said, "I am the resurrection and the life." Lord, you comforted Martha and Mary in their distress; draw near to us who mourn for _____, and dry the tears of those who weep.

> *People:* **Hear us, Lord.**

Leader: You wept at the grave of Lazarus, your friend; comfort us in our sorrow.

> *People:* **Hear us, Lord.**

Leader: You raised the dead to life; give eternal life to our brother/ sister through the power of your resurrection.

> *People:* **Hear us, Lord.**

Leader: You promised paradise to the thief who repented; we trust you to bring our brother/sister into the joys of heaven.

> *People:* **Hear us, Lord.**

Leader: Our brother/sister was washed in baptism and nourished at your table; may we see him/her through the eyes of faith in the fellowship of your saints in glory.

> *People:* **Hear us, Lord.**

Leader: Comfort us in our sorrows; let our faith be our consolation and eternal life our hope, through Jesus Christ our Lord.

A time of silent prayer may be offered.

Leader: We pray this through Christ our Lord.*

> *People:* **Amen.**

   Or

Leader: God of all grace, you sent your Son, our Lord Jesus Christ, to bring life and immortality into the world. We give you thanks that by his death he destroyed the grip of death and by his resurrection he opened the kingdom of God to all believers. Make us confident that because he lives we shall also live. Deepen our conviction that neither death nor life, nor things present nor things to come, nor anything else in all creation shall be able to separate us from your love. Immerse us now in that love, which is in Christ Jesus, our Lord, who lives with you and the Holy Spirit, one God, now and forever.

> *People:* **Amen.**

The prayer(s) may conclude with a commendation.

Commendation

Leader: Into your hands, O merciful Savior, we commend your servant
_____ . Acknowledge, we humbly pray, a sheep of your own

* From *The Book of Common Prayer.*

fold, a lamb of your flock, a sinner of your own redeeming. Receive him/her into the arms of your mercy, into the blessed rest of everlasting peace, and into the glorious company of the saints in light.*

People: **Amen.**

Or

Leader: Holy God, by your creative power you gave us the gift of life, and by your redeeming grace you gave us new life in Jesus Christ. We commend _____ to your merciful keeping through faith in Jesus Christ our Lord whose death saved us from sin and whose resurrection brings us eternal life.

People: **Amen.**

The Lord's Prayer

When the Lord's Prayer is used at the end of the prayer(s), the prayer(s) will be closed with these words: "through Jesus Christ our Lord who taught us to pray, saying . . ."

All: Our Father which art in heaven, hallowed be thy name. Thy kingdom come, Thy will be done on earth, as it is in heaven. Give us this day our daily bread. And forgive us our debts, as we forgive our debtors. And lead us not into temptation, but deliver us from evil: For thine is the kingdom, and the power, and the glory, for ever. Amen. (KJV)

* From *The Book of Common Prayer.*

Or

All: Our Father in heaven, hallowed be your name, your kingdom come, your will be done, on earth as it is in heaven. Give us today our daily bread. And forgive us our debts, as we also have forgiven our debtors. And lead us not into temptation, but deliver us from the evil one. For yours is the kingdom and the power and the glory forever. Amen. (NIV)

Benediction

Leader: "Go in peace, and may the God of peace, who through the blood of the eternal covenant brought back from the dead our Lord Jesus, that great Shepherd of the sheep, equip you with everything good for doing his will, and may he work in us what is pleasing to him, through Jesus Christ, to whom be glory forever and ever" (Heb. 13:20–21).

People: **Amen.**

Or

Leader: May God in his infinite love and mercy bring the whole church, living and departed in the Lord Jesus, to a joyful resurrection and the fulfillment of God's eternal kingdom.

People: **Amen.**

Hymn and Recessional

At a funeral, the casket should be removed from the church (chapel). The minister and family members may precede or follow the casket. The congregation should sing a triumphant hymn during the recessional. At a memorial service, the congregation should sing a triumphant hymn after the benediction closing the service.

Leonard J. Vander Zee, ed., *In Life and in Death* (Grand Rapids: CRC Publications, 1992), 104–20. All rights reserved. Used by permission.

4

Church of the Nazarene

Opening Words

Dearly beloved: We are gathered today to pay our final tribute of respect to that which was mortal of our deceased loved one and friend. To you members of the family who mourn your loss, we especially offer our deep and sincere sympathy. May we share with you the comfort afforded by God's Word for such a time as this.

"Let not your heart be troubled: ye believe in God, believe also in me. In my Father's house are many mansions: if it were not so, I would have told you. I go to prepare a place for you. And if I go and prepare a place for you, I will come again, and receive you unto myself; that where I am, there ye may be also" (John 14:1–3 KJV).

"I am the resurrection, and the life: he that believeth in me, though he were dead, yet shall he live: and whosoever liveth and believeth in me shall never die" (John 11:25–26 KJV).

Invocation

Prayer in the minister's own words or may use the following.

Almighty God, our heavenly Father, we come into this sanctuary of sorrow realizing our utter dependence upon thee. We know thou dost love us and canst turn even the shadow of death into the light of morning. Help us now to wait before thee with reverent and submissive hearts.

Thou art our refuge and strength, O God—a very present help in time of trouble. Grant unto us thy abundant mercy. May those who mourn today find comfort and healing balm in thy sustaining grace. We humbly bring these petitions in the name of our Lord Jesus Christ. Amen.

A Hymn or Special Song

Selections of Scripture

Psalm 27:3–5, 11, 13–14	Matthew 5:3, 4, 6, 8
Psalm 46:1–6, 10–11	1 Peter 1:3–9

Message

A Hymn or Special Song

Closing Prayer

At the Graveside

When the people have assembled, the minister may read any or all of the following Scriptures.

"For I know that my redeemer liveth, and that he shall stand at the latter day upon the earth: and though after my skin worms destroy this body, yet in my flesh shall I see God: whom I shall see for myself, and mine eyes shall behold, and not another" (Job 19:25–27 KJV).

"Behold, I show you a mystery; we shall not all sleep, but we shall all be changed, in a moment, in the twinkling of an eye, at the last trump: for the trumpet shall sound, and the dead shall be raised incorruptible, and we shall be changed. . . . Then shall be brought to pass the saying that is written, Death is swallowed up in victory. O death, where is thy sting? O grave, where is thy victory? The sting of death is sin; and the strength of sin is the law. But thanks be to God, which giveth us the victory through our Lord Jesus Christ.

"Therefore, my beloved brethren, be ye steadfast, unmoveable, always abounding in the work of the Lord, forasmuch as ye know that your labour is not in vain in the Lord" (1 Cor. 15:51–52, 54–58 KJV).

"I heard a voice from heaven saying unto me, Write, Blessed are the dead which die in the Lord from henceforth: Yea, saith the Spirit, that they may rest from their labours; and their works do follow them" (Rev. 14:13 KJV).

The minister shall then read one of the following committal statements.

For a Believer

Forasmuch as the spirit of our departed loved one has returned to God, who gave it, we therefore tenderly commit his/her body to the grave in sure trust and certain hope of the resurrection of the dead and the life of the world to come, through our Lord Jesus Christ, who shall give to us new bodies like unto his glorious body. "Blessed are the dead which die in the Lord."

For a Nonbeliever

We have come now to commit the body of our departed friend to its kindred dust. The spirit we leave with God, for we know the merciful judge of all the earth will do right. Let us who remain dedicate ourselves anew to live in the fear and love of God, so that we may obtain an abundant entrance into the heavenly Kingdom.

For a Child

In the sure and certain hope of the resurrection to eternal life through our Lord Jesus Christ, we commit the body of this child to the grave. And as Jesus, during his earthly life, took the children into his arms and blessed them, may he receive this dear one unto himself, for, as he said, "Of such is the kingdom of heaven."

Prayer

Our heavenly Father, God of all mercy, we look to thee in this moment of sorrow and bereavement. Comfort these dear ones whose hearts are heavy and sad. Wilt thou be with them, sustain and guide them in the days to come. Grant, O Lord, that they may love and serve thee and obtain the fullness of thy promises in the world to come.

"Now the God of peace, that brought again from the dead our Lord Jesus, that great shepherd of the sheep, through the blood of the everlasting covenant, make you perfect in every good work to do his will, working in you that which is well-pleasing in his sight, through Jesus Christ; to whom be glory for ever and ever. Amen" (Heb. 13:20–21 KJV).

Manual: 1993–97 Church of the Nazarene (Kansas City, MO: Nazarene Publishing House, 1993), 248–52. Used by permission.

5

Episcopal

Singing

All stand while one or more of the following anthems are sung or said. A hymn, psalm, or some other suitable anthem may be used instead.

> I am Resurrection and I am Life, says the Lord.
> Whoever has faith in me shall have life,
> even though he die.
> And everyone who has life,
> and has committed himself to me in faith,
> shall not die for ever.
>
> As for me, I know that my Redeemer lives
> and that at the last he will stand upon the earth.
> After my awaking, he will raise me up;
> and in my body I shall see God.

I myself shall see, and my eyes behold him
who is my friend and not a stranger.

For none of us has life in himself,
and none becomes his own master when he dies.
For if we have life, we are alive in the Lord.
So, then, whether we live or die,
we are the Lord's possession.

Happy from now on
are those who die in the Lord!
So it is, says the Spirit,
for they rest from their labors.

Or

In the midst of life we are in death;
from whom can we seek help?
From you alone, O Lord,
who by our sins are justly angered.

Holy God, Holy and Mighty,
Holy and merciful Savior,
deliver us not into the bitterness of eternal death.

Lord, you know the secrets of our hearts;
shut not your ears to our prayers,
but spare us, O Lord.

Holy God, Holy and Mighty,
Holy and merciful Savior,
deliver us not into the bitterness of eternal death.

O worthy and eternal Judge,
do not let the pains of death
turn us away from you at our last hour.

Holy God, Holy and Mighty,
Holy and merciful Savior,
deliver us not into the bitterness of eternal death.

When all are in place, the celebrant may address the congregation, acknowledging briefly the purpose of their gathering and bidding their prayers for the deceased and the bereaved.

The celebrant then says:

The Lord be with you.

People: **And also with you.**

Celebrant: Let us pray.

Silence may be kept, after which the celebrant says one of the following.

Collect

At the Burial of an Adult

O God, who by the glorious resurrection of your Son Jesus Christ destroyed death and brought life and immortality to light: grant that your servant _____, being raised with him, may know the strength of his presence, and rejoice in his eternal glory; who with you and the Holy Spirit lives and reigns, one God, for ever and ever. Amen.

Or

O God, whose mercies cannot be numbered: accept our prayers on behalf of your servant _____, and grant him/her an entrance into the land of light and joy, in the fellowship of your saints; through Jesus Christ our Lord, who lives and reigns with you and the Holy Spirit, one God, now and for ever. Amen.

Or

O God of grace and glory, we remember before you this day our brother/sister _____. We thank you for giving him/her to us, his/her family and friends, to know and to love as a companion on our earthly pilgrimage. In your boundless compassion, console us who mourn. Give us faith to see in death the gate of eternal life, so that in quiet confidence we may continue our course on earth, until, by your call, we are reunited with those who have gone before, through Jesus Christ our Lord. Amen.

At the Burial of a Child

O God, whose beloved Son took children into his arms and blessed them: give us grace to entrust _____ to your never-failing care and love, and bring us all to your heavenly kingdom, through Jesus Christ our Lord, who lives and reigns with you and the Holy Spirit, one God, now and for ever. Amen.

The celebrant may add the following prayer.

Most merciful God, whose wisdom is beyond our understanding: deal graciously with _____'s family and friends in their grief. Surround them with your love, that they may not be overwhelmed by their loss but have confidence in your goodness and strength to meet the days to come, through Jesus Christ our Lord. Amen.

The people sit.

One or more of the following passages from Holy Scripture is read. If there is to be a Communion, a passage from the Gospel always concludes the readings.

The Liturgy of the Word

Old Testament

Job 19:21–27a   Isaiah 25:6–9

Lamentations 3:22–26, 31–33   Isaiah 61:1–3

A suitable psalm, hymn, or canticle may follow. The following Psalms are appropriate: 42:1–7; 46; 90; 112; 121; 130; 139:1–11.

New Testament

Romans 8:14–19, 34–35, 37–39   1 John 3:1–2

1 Corinthians 15:20–26, 35–38, 42, 44, 53–58   Revelation 7:9–17

2 Corinthians 4:16–5:9   Revelation 21:2–7

A suitable psalm, hymn, or canticle may follow. The following Psalms are appropriate: 23; 27; 106:1–5; 116.

Gospel

Then, all standing, the deacon or minister appointed reads the Gospel, first saying:

The Holy Gospel of our Lord Jesus Christ according to John.

> *People:* **Glory to you, Lord Christ.**

John 5:24–27   John 11:21–27

John 6:37–40   John 14:1–6

John 10:11–16

At the end of the Gospel, the reader says:

The Gospel of the Lord.

> *People:* **Praise to you, Lord Christ.**

Here there may be a homily by the celebrant, a member of the family, or a friend.

Apostles' Creed

The Apostles' Creed may then be said, all standing. The celebrant may introduce the creed with the following or similar words.

In the assurance of eternal life, let us proclaim our faith and say,

I believe in God, the Father almighty,
> creator of heaven and earth.

I believe in Jesus Christ, his only Son, our Lord.
> He was conceived by the power of the Holy Spirit and
> > born of the Virgin Mary.
> He suffered under Pontius Pilate,
> > was crucified, died, and was buried.
> He descended to the dead.
> On the third day he rose again.
> He ascended into heaven,
> > and is seated at the right hand of the Father.
> He will come again to judge the living and the dead.

I believe in the Holy Spirit,
> the holy catholic Church,
> the communion of saints,
> the forgiveness of sins,
> the resurrection of the body,
> and the life everlasting. Amen.

If there is not to be a Communion, the Lord's Prayer is said here, and the service continues with the Prayers of the People or with one or more suitable prayers.

When there is a Communion, the following form of the Prayers of the People is used.

The Prayers of the People

Celebrant: For our brother/sister _____, let us pray to our Lord Jesus Christ who said, "I am Resurrection and I am Life."

Lord, you consoled Martha and Mary in their distress; draw near to us who mourn for _____ and dry the tears of those who weep.

> *People:* **Hear us, Lord.**

Celebrant: You wept at the grave of Lazarus, your friend; comfort us in our sorrow.

> *People:* **Hear us, Lord.**

Celebrant: You raised the dead to life; give to our brother/sister eternal life.

> *People:* **Hear us, Lord.**

Celebrant: You promised paradise to the thief who repented; bring our brother/sister to the joys of heaven.

> *People:* **Hear us, Lord.**

Celebrant: Comfort us in our sorrows at the death of our brother/sister; let our faith be our consolation, and eternal life our hope.

Silence may be kept. The celebrant then concludes with one of the following or some other prayer.

Lord Jesus Christ, we commend to you our brother/sister _____, who was reborn by water and the Spirit. Grant that his/her death may recall to us your victory over death, and be an occasion for us to renew our trust in our Father's love. Give us, we pray, the faith to follow where you have led the way, and where you live and reign with the Father and the Holy Spirit, to the ages of ages. Amen.

Or

Father of all, we pray to you for _____, and for all those whom we love but see no longer. Grant to them eternal rest. Let light perpetual shine upon them. May his/her soul and the souls of all the departed, through the mercy of God, rest in peace. Amen.

When there is no Communion, the service continues with the commendation or with the committal.

At the Eucharist

The service continues with the peace and the offertory.

Preface of the Commemoration of the Dead

In place of the usual post-Communion prayer, the following is said.

Almighty God, we thank you that in your great love you have fed us with the spiritual food and drink of the body and blood of your Son Jesus Christ and have given us a foretaste of your heavenly banquet. Grant that this sacrament may be to us a comfort in affliction and a pledge of our inheritance in that kingdom where there is no death, neither sorrow nor crying, but the fullness of joy with all your saints, through Jesus Christ our Savior. Amen.

If the body is not present, the service continues with the (blessing and) dismissal. Unless the committal follows immediately in the church, the following commendation is used.

The Commendation

The celebrant and other ministers take their places at the body. This anthem or some other suitable anthem, or a hymn, may be sung or said.

> Give rest, O Christ, to your servant with your saints,
> where sorrow and pain are no more,
> neither sighing, but life everlasting.

You only are immortal, the creator and maker of mankind; and we are mortal, formed of the earth, and to earth shall we return. For so did you ordain when you created us, saying, "You are dust, and to dust you shall return." All of us go down to the dust; yet even at the grave we make our song: Alleluia, alleluia, alleluia.

> Give rest, O Christ, to your servant with your saints,
> where sorrow and pain are no more,
> neither sighing, but life everlasting.

The celebrant, facing the body, says:

Into your hands, O merciful Savior, we commend your servant
_____ . Acknowledge, we humbly beseech you, a sheep of your own fold, a lamb of your own flock, a sinner of your own redeeming. Receive him/her into the arms of your mercy, into the blessed rest

of everlasting peace, and into the glorious company of the saints in light. Amen.

The celebrant may then bless the people, and a deacon or other minister may dismiss them, saying:

Let us go forth in the name of Christ. Thanks be to God.

As the body is borne from the church, a hymn or one or more of the following anthems may be sung or said.

Christ is risen from the dead, trampling down death by death, and giving life to those in the tomb.

The Sun of Righteousness is gloriously risen, giving light to those who sat in darkness and in the shadow of death.

The Lord will guide our feet into the way of peace, having taken away the sin of the world.

Christ will open the kingdom of heaven to all who believe in his Name, saying, Come, O blessed of my Father; inherit the kingdom prepared for you.

Into paradise may the angels lead you. At your coming may the martyrs receive you, and bring you into the holy city Jerusalem.

The Committal

The following anthem is sung or said.

> Everyone the Father gives to me will come to me;
> I will never turn away anyone who believes in me.
>
> He who raised Jesus Christ from the dead
> will also give new life to our mortal bodies
> through his indwelling Spirit.
>
> My heart, therefore, is glad, and my spirit rejoices;
> my body also shall rest in hope.
>
> You will show me the path of life;
> in your presence there is fullness of joy,
> and in your right hand are pleasures for evermore.

Then, while earth is cast upon the coffin, the celebrant says:

In sure and certain hope of the resurrection to eternal life through our Lord Jesus Christ, we commend to almighty God our brother/sister
_____, and we commit his/her body to the ground; earth to earth, ashes to ashes, dust to dust. The Lord bless him/her and keep him/her, the Lord make his face to shine upon him/her and be gracious to him/her, the Lord lift up his countenance upon him/her and give him/her peace. Amen.

Celebrant: The Lord be with you.

> *People:* **And also with you.**

Celebrant: Let us pray.

All:

> Our Father, who art in heaven,
>   hallowed be thy Name,
>   thy kingdom come,
>   thy will be done,
>   on earth as it is in heaven.
> Give us this day our daily bread.
> And forgive us our trespasses,
>   as we forgive those
>   who trespass against us.
> And lead us not into temptation,
>   but deliver us from evil.
> For thine is the kingdom,
>   and the power, and the glory,
>   for ever and ever. Amen.

Other prayers may be added. Then may be said:

Rest eternal grant to him/her, O Lord; and let light perpetual shine upon him/her. May his/her soul, and the souls of all the departed, through the mercy of God, rest in peace. Amen.

The celebrant dismisses the people with the following words.

Alleluia. Christ is risen.

People: **Thanks be to God.**

Or

The God of peace, that brought again from the dead our Lord Jesus Christ, the great shepherd of the sheep, through the blood of the everlasting covenant, make you perfect in every good work to do his will, working in you that which is well-pleasing in his sight, through Jesus Christ; to whom be glory for ever and ever. Amen.

The Book of Common Prayer, 1979, 491–503.

6

Evangelical Covenant Church

It is appropriate that members of the church be buried from the church. If the service is held in another location, the minister will make such modifications of the order as he or she considers necessary. Before the service begins the casket shall be closed, and it shall remain closed thereafter. Music selected for the service should be of high quality, reflecting the Christian affirmations of trust and confidence in God, comfort, the communion of saints, and hope in the resurrection. If the family prefers, the committal service may take place before the service at the church. In either case, the following order may be used.

Prelude

Call to Worship

Let us worship God and remember before him his servant _____.
In the name of the Father, the Son, and the Holy Spirit. Amen.

Then one or more of the following sentences may be read.

Blessed be the God and Father of our Lord Jesus Christ, the Father of mercies and the God of all consolation. He comforts us in all our sorrows so that we can comfort others in their sorrows with the consolation we ourselves have received from God (2 Cor. 1:3–4).

Jesus said: I am the resurrection and the life. If anyone believes in me, even though he die he will live, and whoever lives and believes in me will never die (John 11:25–26).

Come to me, all you who labor and are overburdened, and I will give you rest (Matt. 11:28).

"Our help is in the name of the LORD, who made heaven and earth" (Ps. 124:8 RSV).

Invocation

Almighty God, whose love never fails and who can turn the shadow of death into daybreak: help us to receive your Word with believing hearts, so that, hearing the promises in Scripture, we may have hope and be lifted out of darkness into the light and peace of your presence, through Jesus Christ our Lord. Amen.

Or

O God of grace and glory, we remember before you today our brother/ sister _____. We thank you for giving him/her to us to know and to love as a companion of our pilgrimage on earth. In your bound-less compassion, console us who mourn. Give us your aid so we may see in death the gate to eternal life, that we may continue our course on earth in confidence until, by your call, we are reunited with those who have gone before us, through your Son, Jesus Christ our Lord. Amen.

Or

Our Father in heaven, whose love is infinite and in whose will is our peace: be pleased to look upon our sorrow, and enable us so to hear your holy Word that through patience and the comfort of the Scriptures we may be raised above the shadows of mortality into the light of your countenance and the joy of your presence, through him who died and rose again and ever lives with you, even Jesus Christ our Lord. Amen.

Hymn

Scripture Lessons

Let us hear the Word of God.

Psalms

Psalm 23	Psalm 118:5, 8, 9, 13, 15–17, 19, 20
Psalm 42	Psalm 121
Psalm 46	Psalm 130
Psalm 90:1–12	Psalm 139:1–17, 22, 28
Psalm 103	

Old Testament

Job 14

Isaiah 25:6–9

Isaiah 40:1–11

Isaiah 40:28–31

Isaiah 61:1–3

Lamentations 3:22–26, 31–33

Gospel

Matthew 11:25–30

Luke 12:25–40

John 5:24–29

John 6:37–40

John 10:11–16

John 11:17–27

John 14:1–6

John 14:15–21

Epistle

Romans 8:14–19, 31–35, 37–39

1 Corinthians 15:3–8, 12–20, 35–38, 42–50

2 Corinthians 4:12–5:9

1 Thessalonians 4:13–18

1 Peter 1:3–9

1 John 3:1–2

Revelation 7:9–17

Revelation 21:2–7

At the burial of a child the following Scriptures may be read.

Matthew 18:1–5, 10–14

Mark 10:13–16

Following the reading of the Scriptures, there may be a brief tribute or obituary.

Pastoral Prayer

O God, before whom generations rise and pass away: we praise you for all your servants who, having lived this life in faith, now live eternally with you. Especially we thank you for your servant _____, for the gift of his/her life that was good and kind and faithful. (*Here mention may be made of characteristics or service.*) We thank you that for him/her death is past and pain is ended, and he/she has entered the joy you have prepared.

Stand by those in sorrow that, as they lean on your strength, they may be upheld and comforted by the good news of the life of the world to come. Give us faith to see, beyond touch and sight, some sign of your kingdom and, where vision fails, to trust your love that never fails. Lift heavy sorrow and give us good hope in Jesus, so we may bravely walk our earthly way and look forward to glad heavenly reunion, through Jesus Christ our Lord, who was dead but is risen, to whom we give honor and praise, now and forever. Amen.

Hymn

Sermon

While the sermon may include appropriate recognition of the life of the deceased, let there be a clear witness to the resurrection and our hope and comfort in Christ.

Affirmation of Faith

The Apostles' Creed may be used.

I believe in God, the Father almighty, creator of heaven and earth.

I believe in Jesus Christ, his only Son, our Lord. He was conceived by the power of the Holy Spirit, and born of the Virgin Mary. He suffered under Pontius Pilate, was crucified, died, and was buried. He descended to the dead. On the third day he rose again. He ascended into heaven, and is seated at the right hand of the Father. He will come again to judge the living and the dead.

I believe in the Holy Spirit, the holy catholic Church, the communion of saints, the forgiveness of sin, the resurrection of the body, and the life everlasting. Amen.

Instead of the Apostles' Creed, the following affirmation may be used.

We believe there is no condemnation for those who are in Christ Jesus: and we know that in everything God works for good with those who love him, and who are called according to his purpose. We are sure that neither death, nor life, nor angels, nor principalities, nor things present, nor things to come, nor powers, nor height, nor depth, nor anything else in all creation, will be able to separate us from the love of God in Christ Jesus our Lord. Amen.

Hymn

This should be a hymn of thanksgiving.

Benediction

The peace of God, which passes all understanding, will keep your hearts and your minds in Christ Jesus. Amen.

Or

The grace of the Lord Jesus Christ, and the love of God, and the fellowship of the Holy Spirit, be with you all. Amen.

As the procession leaves the church, the Nunc Dimittis may be said by the minister.

Lord, now lettest thou thy servant depart in peace, according to thy word; for mine eyes have seen thy salvation, which thou hast prepared before the face of all people, to be a light to lighten the Gentiles, and to be the glory of thy people, Israel.

Glory to the Father, and to the Son, and to the Holy Spirit; as it was in the beginning, is now, and will be for ever. Amen.

The Covenant Book of Worship (Chicago: Covenant Press, 1978), 186–213. Used by permission.

7

Evangelical Free Church of America

Prelude

Invocation

Eternal God, our heavenly Father, who loves us with an everlasting love, and can turn the shadow of death into the morning: help us now to wait upon you with reverent and believing hearts. In the silence of this hour speak to us of eternal things, that through patience and the comfort of the Scriptures we may have hope and be lifted above our darkness and distress into the light and peace of your presence, through Jesus Christ our Lord. Amen.

Extemporaneous Prayer

Recognize God's love, care, and wisdom

Give thanks for the Christian's hope of eternal life in Christ

Give thanks for memories of the deceased

Invoke God's help and a sense of his presence in this service

Welcome

If you are unknown to the guests, introduce yourself. On behalf of the family, thank those who have come.

Song (optional)

Sung by congregation or soloist.

Scripture

Psalm 23	John 14:1–6
Psalm 61:1–5	2 Corinthians 5:1–2
Isaiah 57:1–2	1 Thessalonians 4:13–18
Isaiah 57:15	Revelation 1:17–18
Lamentations 3:19–26, 31–33	Revelation 21:1–4
John 11:25–26	

Other Scripture

There are, of course, scores of hope-filled and comforting texts in Scripture. Following are but a few more.

Job 19:25–26	John 14:27
Psalm 16	Romans 8
Psalm 39	Romans 14:7–9
Psalm 42	1 Corinthians 15
Psalm 46	2 Corinthians 4:17–18
Psalm 57	Philippians 3:20–21
Psalm 90	2 Timothy 4:6–8
Psalm 130	Hebrews 12:1–3
Matthew 11:28–30	Revelation 7:9–17
John 11:17–27	Revelation 22:1–5

Song (optional)

Sung by congregation or soloist.

Obituary and Eulogy

Beyond the pastor's comments, specially prepared tributes from friends or family may be included at this point. With the permission of the family, extemporaneous words of appreciation and remembrance may be invited from those gathered.

Sermon

Optional: affirmation of faith (such as the Apostles' Creed).

Prayer

Lord and master, you are touched with the feeling of our sorrows. Fulfill your promise that you will not leave your people comfortless but will come to them. Reveal your tender love and grace to your grieving servants and cause them to hear you say, "I am the resurrection and the life." Help them, O Lord, to turn to you in true faith, that, finding now the comfort of your presence, they may also have a sure confidence in you for all that is to come, until the day breaks and these shadows flee away. In your name, O Lord our God and Savior, we pray. Amen.

Extemporaneous Prayer

> Reflect on the message just preached, applying its truths to the listeners
>
> Thank God again for the memory of this loved one and for the promise of our hope in Christ
>
> Ask for God's ongoing comfort

Benediction

Choose one or more of the following selections.

May the peace of God, which transcends all understanding, guard your hearts and your minds in Christ Jesus (Phil. 4:7).

Or: May the peace of God, which passes all understanding, keep your hearts and minds in the knowledge and love of God and His Son,

Jesus Christ our Lord, and may the blessing of God almighty, the Father, the Son, and the Holy Spirit be upon you.

Or

May the grace of the Lord Jesus Christ, and the love of God, and the fellowship of the Holy Spirit be with you all (2 Cor. 13:14).

Or

May the God of all grace, who called you to his eternal glory in Christ, after you have suffered a little while, himself restore you and make you strong, firm and steadfast. To him be the power for ever and ever. Amen (1 Pet. 5:10–11).

Or

Now may the Lord Jesus Christ be with you, for he came to bind up the brokenhearted, comfort all who mourn, and provide for those who grieve. He has promised to grant you a crown of beauty instead of ashes, the oil of joy instead of mourning, and a garment of praise instead of a spirit of despair. Go in his peace. Amen (Isa. 61:1–3).

Or

This is God's word for you: "Do not fear, for I have redeemed you; I have summoned you by name; you are mine. When you pass through the waters, I will be with you; and when you pass through the rivers, they will not sweep over you. When you walk through the fire, you will not be burned; the flames will not set you ablaze. For I am the LORD your God, the Holy One of Israel, your Savior" (Isa. 43:1–3).

Or

"May the God of peace, who through the blood of the eternal covenant brought back from the dead our Lord Jesus, that great Shepherd of the sheep, equip you with everything good for doing his will, and may he work in us what is pleasing to him, through Jesus Christ, to whom be glory for ever and ever. Amen" (Heb. 13:20–21).

Alternate benedictions may be drawn from Romans 8:38–39; 1 Peter 1:3–4; Jude 24–25.

At the conclusion of the service, the funeral director will give instructions to the congregation and guide the dismissal of family members.

Postlude

It is customary for the pastor to lead the pallbearers to the funeral coach, and from the funeral coach to the burial site. Check with the funeral director for local customs.

The Graveside Service (Interment) of a Believer

This is a very brief service at the graveside or mausoleum. Occasionally, this service is not actually held at the graveside (due to inclement weather, for instance, or the difficulty that the elderly may have in walking to the grave site). This element is sometimes incorporated at the conclusion of the funeral itself, so that both services happen in one place and time.

The pastor shall precede the pallbearers to the grave. After the casket has been positioned over the grave, at the signal of the funeral director, the pastor shall stand at the head or behind the casket to perform the committal.

Scripture

See selections above.

Committal

Forasmuch as it has pleased our heavenly Father in his wise providence to take unto himself our beloved _____, we therefore commit his/her body to the ground, earth to earth, ashes to ashes, dust to dust, looking for the blessed hope and glorious appearing of our great God and Savior Jesus Christ. He will change this decaying body and fashion it anew in the likeness of his own glorious resurrection body. He will do this by unleashing his mighty power by which he is able to bring all things under his dominion.

(*Or, in the event of an "untimely" death*) For reasons beyond our understanding it has pleased our wise and good heavenly Father to take to himself this precious loved one and friend, _____. Therefore, we surrender him/her to the Lord who gave him/her to us and to whom he/she was dedicated in life and in death. Here we commit his/her body to the earth, knowing that _____ does not lie in this tomb, but rather is in the presence of God.

In letting _____ go, we affirm our confidence in the blessed hope and glorious appearing of our great God and Savior Jesus Christ, who has promised to give him/her a new resurrection body as different from this as the flower is from the seed, and we rest in the confidence that all who know Christ will be reunited forever in heaven, where there are no more tears, where the atmosphere resounds with praise, and where God himself is the light. Amen.

During the phrase, "earth to earth," and so on, the pastor may sprinkle dirt upon the casket. Another option is to use flowers. Check on local customs.

Benediction

See selections above.

Lee Eclov, ed., *Pastor's Service Manual* (Minneapolis: Free Church Publications, 2011), 120–25. Used by permission.

8

Free Methodist

Musical Prelude

Opening Scriptural Sentences

"I am the resurrection and the life; he who believes in me, though he die, yet shall he live, and whoever lives and believes in me shall never die" (John 11:25–26 RSV).

"For this slight momentary affliction is preparing for us an eternal weight of glory beyond all comparison, because we look not to the things that are seen but to the things that are unseen; for the things that are seen are transient, but the things that are unseen are eternal" (2 Cor. 4:17–18 RSV).

Invocation

O Eternal God, our Father, from whom we come and to whom we go, grant us the favor of your divine presence at this time in our earthly pilgrimage; assure us by your Spirit that the one we serve, even Jesus, has conquered death and is alive forevermore; enable us to view our temporal lives in the light of the eternal; and so may our spirits grow calm and our vision clear, through Christ we pray. Amen.

Hymn (optional)

Sung or played by the congregation, musicians, or organist.

Obituary and/or Tributes

Old Testament Scriptures

Numbers 23:10	Psalm 90
Psalm 23	Psalm 91:1–2
Psalm 27:1	Psalm 103:13
Psalm 42:11	Psalm 121
Psalm 46:1–2	Psalm 124:8

Hymn (optional)

Sung or played by the congregation, musicians, or organist.

Meditation

Prayer for the Family and Community

Benediction

Not used if the service is to continue at the graveside.

Committal Service at Cemetery

Scripture

Job 1:21

John 11:25–26

John 14:1–6

John 19:25–27

1 Timothy 6:7

Words of Committal

Inasmuch as almighty God, in his wise providence, has taken out of this world our deceased brother/sister/child, we therefore commit this mortal body to the ground, looking for the general resurrection in the last day and the life of the world to come, through our Lord Jesus Christ, at whose second coming in glorious majesty to judge the world, the earth and the sea shall give up their dead; and the corruptible bodies of those who sleep in him shall be changed, and made like unto his own glorious body, according to the mighty working whereby he is able to subdue all things unto himself.

Prayer

The minister may pray extemporaneously or use one of the following collects.

O merciful God, the Father of our Lord Jesus Christ, who is the resurrection and the life, in whom whosoever believeth shall live, though he die, and whosoever liveth and believeth in him shall not die eternally, we meekly beseech you, O Father, to raise us from the death of sin unto the life of righteousness, that when we shall depart this life we may rest in him, and at the general resurrection on the last day may be found acceptable in your sight and receive that blessing that your well-loved Son shall then pronounce to all who love and fear you, saying, "Come, you blessed of My Father, receive the kingdom prepared for you from the beginning of the world." Grant this, we beseech you, O merciful Father, through Jesus Christ, our Redeemer.

Or

Forasmuch as the spirit of the departed has returned to God who gave it, we therefore commit his/her body to the ground, earth to earth, ashes to ashes, dust to dust; looking for the general resurrection in the last day, and the life of the world to come, through our Lord Jesus Christ; at whose coming in glorious majesty to judge the world, the earth and the sea shall give up their dead; and the corruptible bodies of those who sleep in him shall be changed and made like unto his own glorious body; according to the mighty working whereby he is able to subdue all things unto himself.

Or

Forasmuch as the spirit of this departed loved one has returned to God who gave it, we therefore tenderly commit his/her body to the ground in sure trust and certain hope in the power and love of Christ our Lord; at whose divine call they that sleep in him shall one day rise to stand with him, and hear with all saints the welcome summons: "Enter into your master's joy." For his is the kingdom and the power, and the glory, for ever.

Or for a child

In the sure hope of the resurrection to eternal life through our Lord Jesus Christ, we commit the body of this child to the ground. The Lord bless him/her and keep him/her, the Lord make his face to shine upon him/her and be gracious unto him/her, the Lord lift up his countenance upon him/her and give him/her peace, both now and evermore.

Benediction

The grace of our Lord Jesus Christ, and the love of God, and the fellowship of the Holy Spirit, be with you all evermore. Amen.

Clyde E. Van Valin, ed., *Pastor's Handbook* (Indianapolis: Free Methodist Publishing House, 1994), 157–60. Used by permission.

9

Lutheran

This rite may be used as a memorial service by omitting those portions indicated by "(•)" on the left. At the entrance to the church, the ministers meet the coffin, the pallbearers, and the bereaved.

Entrance

Pastor: Blessed be the God and Father of our Lord Jesus Christ, the source of all mercy and the God of all consolation. He comforts us in all our sorrows so that we can comfort others in their sorrows with the consolation we ourselves have received from God.

> *Congregation:* **Thanks be to God.**

A pall may be placed upon the coffin by the pallbearers or other assisting ministers, and the following may be said.

Pastor: When we were baptized in Christ Jesus, we were baptized into his death. We were buried therefore with him by baptism into death, so that as Christ was raised from the dead by the glory of the Father, we too might live a new life. For if we have been united with him in a death like his, we shall certainly be united with him in a resurrection like his.

(•) *Stand. The procession forms and enters the church, the ministers preceding the coffin. A psalm, hymn, or appropriate verse may be sung as the procession goes to the front of the church.*

The Liturgy of the Word

Pastor: The Lord be with you.

> *Congregation:* **And also with you.**

Pastor: Let us pray.

O God of grace and glory, we remember before you today our brother/sister _____ . We thank you for giving him/her to us to know and to love as a companion in our pilgrimage on earth. In your boundless compassion, console us who mourn. Give us your aid, so we may see in death the gate to eternal life, that we may continue our course on earth in confidence until, by your call, we are reunited with those who have gone before us, through your Son, Jesus Christ our Lord.

> *Congregation:* **Amen.**

Or

Pastor: Almighty God, source of all mercy and giver of comfort: deal graciously, we pray, with those who mourn, that, casting all their sorrow on you, they may know the consolation of your love, through your Son, Jesus Christ our Lord.

> *Congregation:* **Amen.**

Or

Pastor: Almighty God, those who die in the Lord still live with you in joy and blessedness. We give you heartfelt thanks for the grace you have bestowed upon your servants who have finished their course in faith and now rest from their labors. May we, with all who have died in the true faith, have perfect fulfillment and joy in your eternal and everlasting glory, through your Son, Jesus Christ our Lord.

> *Congregation:* **Amen.**

Or

Pastor: O God, your days are without end and your mercies cannot be counted. Make us aware of the shortness and uncertainty of human life, and let your Holy Spirit lead us in holiness and righteousness all the days of our life, so that, when we shall have served you in our generation, we may be gathered to our ancestors, having the testimony of a good conscience, in the communion of your church, in the confidence of a certain faith, in the comfort of a holy hope, in favor with you, our God, and in peace with all humanity, through Jesus Christ our Lord.

> *Congregation:* **Amen.**

Or at the burial of a child

Pastor: O God our Father, your beloved Son took children into his arms and blessed them. Give us grace, we pray, that we may entrust _____ to your never-failing care and love, and bring us all to your heavenly kingdom, through your Son, Jesus Christ our Lord.

> *Congregation:* **Amen.**

Sit. One or two lessons are read. A psalm, hymn, or anthem may be sung between the first and second readings. The appropriate verse may be sung.

> *Congregation:* **Alleluia, Jesus Christ is the firstborn of the dead; to him be glory and power forever and ever. Amen. Alleluia.**

Or during Lent

> *Congregation:* **If we have died with Christ, we shall also live with him; if we are faithful to the end, we shall reign with him.**

Stand. The Gospel is read.
Sit. The sermon follows the reading of the Gospel.
Stand. A hymn is sung. The Apostles' Creed may be said.

Pastor: God has made us his people through our baptism into Christ. Living together in trust and hope, we confess our faith.

All: I believe in God, the Father almighty, creator of heaven and earth.

I believe in Jesus Christ, his only Son, our Lord. He was conceived by the power of the Holy Spirit and born of the Virgin Mary. He suffered under Pontius Pilate, was crucified, died, and was buried. He descended into hell. (Or, he descended to the dead.) On the third day he rose again. He ascended into heaven, and is seated at the right hand of the Father. He will come again to judge the living and the dead.

I believe in the Holy Spirit, the holy catholic Church, the communion of saints, the forgiveness of sins, the resurrection of the body, and the life everlasting. Amen.

The following prayers are said. Other appropriate prayers may be used instead.

Assisting Pastor: Let us pray.

Almighty God, you have knit your chosen people together in one communion, in the mystical body of your Son, Jesus Christ our Lord. Give to your whole church in heaven and on earth your light and your peace.

Congregation: **Hear us, Lord.**

Assisting Pastor: Grant that all who have been baptized into Christ's death and resurrection may die to sin and rise to newness of life and that through the grave and gate of death we may pass with him to our joyful resurrection.

Congregation: **Hear us, Lord.**

Assisting Pastor: Grant to us who are still in our pilgrimage, and who walk as yet by faith, that your Holy Spirit may lead us in holiness and righteousness all our days.

Congregation: **Hear us, Lord.**

Assisting Pastor: Grant to your faithful people pardon and peace, that we may be cleansed from all our sins and serve you with a quiet mind.

Congregation: **Hear us, Lord.**

Assisting Pastor: Grant to all who mourn a sure confidence in your loving care, that, casting all their sorrow on you, they may know the consolation of your love.

Congregation: **Hear us, Lord.**

Assisting Pastor: Give courage and faith to those who are bereaved, that they may have strength to meet the days ahead in the comfort of a holy and certain hope, and in the joyful expectation of eternal life with those they love.

Congregation: **Hear us, Lord.**

Assisting Pastor: Help us, we pray, in the midst of things we cannot understand, to believe and trust in the communion of saints, the forgiveness of sins, and the resurrection to life everlasting.

Congregation: **Hear us, Lord.**

Assisting Pastor: Grant us grace to entrust _____ to your never-failing love that sustained him/her in this life. Receive him/her into the arms of your mercy, and remember him/her according to the favor you bear for your people.

Congregation: **Hear us, Lord.**

The minister concludes the intercessions with one of the following prayers.

Assisting Pastor: God of all grace, you sent your Son, our Savior Jesus Christ, to bring life and immortality to light. We give you thanks because by his death Jesus destroyed the power of death and by his resurrection has opened the kingdom of heaven to all believers. Make us certain that because he lives we shall live also, and that neither death nor life, nor things present nor things to come shall be able to separate us from your love, which is in Christ Jesus our Lord, who lives and reigns with you and the Holy Spirit, one God, now and forever.

Congregation: **Amen.**

Or

Assisting Pastor: God, the generations rise and pass away before you. You are the strength of those who labor; you are the rest of the blessed dead. We rejoice in the company of your saints. We remember all who have lived in faith, all who have peacefully died, and especially those most dear to us who rest in you. . . . Give us in time our portion with those who have trusted in you and have striven to do your holy will.

To your name, with the church on earth and the church in heaven, we ascribe all honor and glory, now and forever.

> *Congregation:* **Amen.**

When Holy Communion is celebrated, the service continues with the peace. The commendation then follows the post-Communion canticle ("Lord, now you let your servant . . .") and prayer.

When there is no Communion, the service continues with the Lord's Prayer.

Our Father in heaven, hallowed be your name, your kingdom come, your will be done, on earth as in heaven. Give us today our daily bread. Forgive us our sins as we forgive those who sin against us. Save us from the time of trial and deliver us from evil. For the kingdom, the power, and the glory are yours now and forever. Amen.

Sit.

(•) Commendation

The ministers take their places at the coffin.

Pastor: Into your hands, O merciful Savior, we commend your servant, _____. Acknowledge, we humbly beseech you, a sheep of your own fold, a lamb of your own flock, a sinner of your own redeeming. Receive him/her into the arms of your mercy, into the blessed rest of everlasting peace, and into the glorious company of the saints in light.

> *Congregation:* **Amen.**

Pastor: Let us go forth in peace.

> *Congregation:* **In the name of Christ. Amen.**

Stand. The procession forms and leaves the church, the ministers preceding the coffin. As the procession leaves the church, a psalm, hymn, or anthem may be sung. The canticle "Lord, now you let your servant . . ." may be sung if it has not been sung during Holy Communion.

Committal

The ministers precede the coffin to the place of interment. During the procession, one or more of the following verses may be sung or said.

Assisting Pastor: I called to the Lord in my distress; the Lord answered by setting me free. It is better to rely on the Lord than to put any trust in flesh. It is better to rely on the Lord than to put any trust in rulers.

I was pressed so hard that I almost fell, but the Lord came to my help.

There is a sound of exultation and victory in the tents of the righteous: "The right hand of the Lord has triumphed! The right hand of the Lord is exalted! The right hand of the Lord has triumphed!"

I shall not die, but live, and declare the works of the Lord.

Open for me the gates of righteousness; I will enter them; I will offer thanks to the Lord. "This is the gate of the Lord; he who is righteous may enter" (adapted from Ps. 118).

Or

Assisting Pastor: "For I know that my Redeemer lives, and at last he will stand upon the earth; and after my skin has been thus destroyed, then from my flesh I shall see God" (Job 19:25–26 RSV).

Or

Assisting Pastor: "None of us lives to himself, and none of us dies to himself. If we live, we live to the Lord, and if we die, we die to the Lord; so then, whether we live or whether we die, we are the Lord's" (Rom. 14:7–8 RSV).

Or

Assisting Pastor: "I am the resurrection and the life," says the Lord; "he who believes in me, though he die, yet shall he live, and whoever lives and believes in me shall never die" (John 11:25–26a RSV).

When all have arrived at the place of burial, the following prayer may be said.

Pastor: Almighty God, by the death and burial of Jesus, your anointed, you have destroyed death and sanctified the graves of all your saints. Keep our brother/sister, whose body we now lay to rest, in the company of all your saints and, at the last, raise him/her up to share with all your faithful people the endless joy and peace won through the glorious resurrection of Christ our Lord, who lives and reigns with you and the Holy Spirit, one God, now and forever.

> *Congregation:* **Amen.**

One of the following lessons may be read.

John 12:23–26   Philippians 3:20–21
1 Corinthians 15:51–57

The coffin is lowered into the grave or placed in its resting place. Earth may be cast on the coffin as the minister says:

Pastor: In sure and certain hope of the resurrection to eternal life through our Lord Jesus Christ, we commend to almighty God our brother/sister _____, and we commit his/her body to the ground/the deep/the elements/its resting place; earth to earth, ashes to ashes, dust to dust. The Lord bless him/her and keep him/her. The Lord make his face shine on him/her and be gracious to him/her. The Lord look upon him/her with favor and give him/her peace.

> *Congregation:* **Amen.**

Or

Pastor: Since almighty God has called our brother/sister _____ from this life to himself, we commit his/her body to the earth from which it was made/the deep/the elements/its resting place. Christ was the first to rise from the dead, and we know that he will raise up our mortal bodies to be like his in glory. We commend our brother/ sister to the Lord: may the Lord receive him/her into his peace and raise him/her up on the last day.

Congregation: **Amen.**

Pastor: Lord, remember us in your kingdom, and teach us to pray:

All: Our Father in heaven, hallowed be your name, your kingdom come, your will be done, on earth as in heaven. Give us today our daily bread. Forgive us our sins as we forgive those who sin against us. Save us from the time of trial and deliver us from evil. For the kingdom, the power, and the glory are yours now and forever. Amen.

Pastor: Lord Jesus, by your death you took away the sting of death. Grant to us your servants, so to follow in faith where you have led the way, that we may at length fall asleep peacefully in you and wake in your likeness; to you, the author and giver of life, be all honor and glory, now and forever.

Congregation: **Amen.**

Then may be said:

Pastor: Rest eternal grant him/her, O Lord;

Assisting Pastor: **And let light perpetual shine upon him/her.**

The minister blesses the people.

Pastor: The God of peace—who brought again from the dead our Lord Jesus Christ, the great shepherd of the sheep, through the blood of the everlasting covenant—make you perfect in every good work to do his will, working in you that which is well-pleasing in his sight, through Jesus Christ, to whom be glory forever and ever.

Congregation: **Amen.**

Pastor: Let us go in peace.

Lutheran Book of Worship (Minneapolis: Augsburg Fortress, 1978), 206–13. Used by permission. May not be reproduced without permission from the publisher.

10

Presbyterian

Scripture

Let the service begin with the reading of the whole or a part of the following selections from Scripture.

1 Chronicles 29:15   John 11:25

Job 1:21   1 Timothy 6:7

Job 14:1

Prayer of Invocation

O God, who art our God, and our fathers' God; thou whose compassions fail not, but who are the same yesterday, today, and forever, grant us now thy presence, we beseech thee, that our souls may be strengthened, and that we faint not under thine afflicting providence, but that through thy condescension we may find all grace to help in this our time of need, which we ask in the name of Jesus Christ, our Lord and Savior, to whom, with thee and the Holy Ghost, we will ascribe all honor, majesty, and might, world without end. Amen.

Hymn

Scripture

Let the whole or a part of the following selections be read.

Psalm 27	Ecclesiastes 12
Psalm 39:4–13	1 Corinthians 15:20–58
Psalm 90:1–12	Revelation 22:1–5

Prayer

Almighty and most merciful God, our heavenly Father, the consolation of the sorrowful and the support of the stricken, who does not willingly afflict the children of men, look in pity, we beseech you, on all upon whom you have laid your afflicting hand, and, in the multitude of your tender mercies, be pleased to uphold and comfort them in the day of their trial and distress. Grant us all grace that we may lay to heart the lesson of this solemn providence, and work while the day lasts, knowing that the night comes, when no man can work; and that we may set our affections on things that are in heaven, and not on things that are on the earth. Enable us to live by faith in the Son of God, that when

Christ, who is our life, shall appear, we also may appear with him in glory.

O Lord Jesus Christ, Son of God, lamb of God, who takes away the sin of the world, to whom shall we go but to you? You have the words of eternal life. You who were a man of sorrows and acquainted with grief, have pity upon those who cry unto you. When our eyes grow dim in the shadows of death, and we pass through the deep waters, by your agony and bloody sweat, and by your death on Calvary, we beseech you to remember us. O you who have saved us, forsake us not in the trying hour; you who has vanquished death, give us the victory and bring us to your own everlasting rest in the assembly of your saints on high.

O God, the Holy Ghost, author of light and life and truth, inspire our souls with hope through the gospel of our Lord Jesus Christ, imparting the benefits of his atonement, and the power of his all-sufficient grace. Release us from our sins; fill us with the fruits of your own indwelling and form us anew in the image of God. Help us now, O blessed comforter; heal our wounded spirits and do not despise our broken and contrite hearts.

O God the Father, God the Son, and God the Holy Spirit, Triune Jehovah, have mercy upon us, your servants, as we wait before you, and hear our prayer. Be pleased graciously to attend to our humble requests and to do for us all that we need, glorifying yourself by us both in this present world, and in that which is to come, all of which we ask through Jesus Christ our Lord. Amen.

Our Father in heaven, hallowed be your name. Your kingdom come. Your will be done on earth, as it is in heaven. Give us this day our daily bread. And forgive us our debts, as we forgive our debtors. And do not lead us into temptation, but deliver us from the evil one: For yours is the kingdom, and the power, and the glory, for ever. Amen.

Benediction

The grace of the Lord Jesus Christ, and the love of God, and the communion of the Holy Spirit, be with you all. Amen.

Hymn

Graveside Service

Words of Introduction

Forasmuch as it has pleased almighty God, in his wise providence, to take out of this world the soul of our deceased brother/sister, we therefore commit his/her body to the ground; earth to earth, ashes to ashes, dust to dust: awaiting the hour when all who are in their graves shall hear the voice of the Son of God, and shall come forth, "they that have done good, unto the resurrection of life; and they that have done evil, unto the resurrection of judgment" (John 5:29 ASV).

"I would not have you to be ignorant, brethren, concerning them which are asleep, that ye sorrow not, even as others which have no hope. For if we believe that Jesus died, and rose again, even so them also which sleep in Jesus will God bring with him" (1 Thess. 4:13 KJV).

"And I heard a voice from heaven saying unto me, Write, Blessed are the dead which die in the Lord from henceforth: Yea, saith the Spirit, that they may rest from their labours; and their works do follow them" (Rev. 14:13 KJV).

Prayers

Almighty God, who has sanctified the grave by thy Son's rest therein, and by his glorious resurrection hast brought life and immortality to light, accept, we pray thee, our unfeigned thanks for the victory that he has obtained for us and for all who sleep in him, and keep us who are still in the body, in everlasting fellowship with all that wait for thee on earth, and with all that are around thee in heaven, in union with him who is the resurrection and the life, who liveth and reigneth with thee and the Holy Ghost, ever one God, world without end. Amen.

O merciful God, the Father of our Lord Jesus Christ, who is the resurrection and the life; in whom whosoever believeth, shall live, though he die; and whosoever liveth and believeth in him, shall not die eternally; who also hath taught us, by his holy apostle Paul, not to be sorry, as men without hope, for those who sleep in him; we humbly beseech thee, O Father, to raise us from the death of sin unto the life of righteousness; that when we shall depart this life, we may rest in him; and that, at the general resurrection in the last day, we may be found acceptable in thy sight; and receive that blessing, which thy well-beloved Son shall then pronounce to all who love and fear thee, saying, come, ye blessed children of my Father, receive the kingdom prepared for you from the beginning of the world. Grant this, we beseech thee O merciful Father, through Jesus Christ, our mediator and redeemer. Amen.*

* From John Knox's liturgy, *Book of Common Order*, 1564.

Benediction

"Now may the God of peace who brought up our Lord Jesus from the dead, that great Shepherd of the sheep, through the blood of the everlasting covenant, make you complete in every good work to do His will, working in you what is well pleasing in His sight, through Jesus Christ, to whom be glory forever and ever. Amen" (Heb. 13:20–21).

The Directory for the Worship of God (Atlanta: Presbyterian Church in America, 2015), appendixes C and E. Used by permission.

11

Reformed Church in America

The Approach to God

Votum

Our help is in the name of the Lord, who made heaven and earth. Amen.

Or

In the name of the Father and of the Son and of the Holy Spirit. Amen.

Sentences

"Come to me, all who labor and are heavy laden, and I will give you rest. Take my yoke upon you, and learn from me; for I am gentle and lowly in heart, and you will find rest for your souls" (Matt. 11:28–29 RSV).

Or

"I am the resurrection and the life," says the Lord; "he who believes in me, though he die, yet shall he live, and whoever lives and believes in me shall never die" (John 11:25–26 RSV).

Another appropriate passage, such as Job 1:21; John 14:25–27; or Romans 14:7–9, may be used.

Salutation

Grace to you and peace from God our Father and the Lord Jesus Christ. Amen.

Or

"Grace to you and peace from him who is and who was and who is to come, . . . and from Jesus Christ the faithful witness, the first-born of the dead, and the ruler of the kings on earth. To him who loves us and has freed us from our sins by his blood and made us a kingdom, priests of his God and Father, to him be glory and dominion for ever and ever. Amen" (Rev. 1:4b–6 RSV).

A hymn may be sung or the service may proceed to the confession or the prayer of illumination.

Prayer of Confession

Eternal God, before whose face the generations rise and pass away, you formed us in your image and willed us to live before you in peace and love. We confess we are not the people you created or called us to be—we have not loved you with our whole heart or our neighbors as ourselves. Forgive us our sin, O God, and create in us a new and willing spirit, so that in our living, we may serve you, and in our dying, we may enter the joy of your presence, through Jesus Christ our Lord.

> *Lord, have mercy upon us.*
> *Christ, have mercy upon us.*
> *Lord, have mercy upon us.*

Assurance of Pardon

"With everlasting love I will have compassion on you, says the LORD your Redeemer. . . . I, I am he who blots out your transgressions for my own sake, and I will not remember your sins. . . . Return to me, for I have redeemed you" (Isa. 54:8; 43:25; 44:22 RSV).

In the name of the Father, and of the Son, and of the Holy Spirit. Amen.

Or

Who is in a position to condemn? Only Christ, and Christ died for us, Christ rose for us, Christ reigns in power for us, Christ prays for us. Hear and believe the good news of the gospel: God is love, and in his love we are forgiven. Amen.

Or

"For God so loved the world that he gave his only Son, that whoever believes in him should not perish but have eternal life. For God sent the Son into the world, not to condemn the world, but that the world might be saved through him" (John 3:16–17 RSV).

May the God and Father of our Lord Jesus Christ pardon all our sins. Amen.

The Word of God

Prayer of Illumination

Let us pray. Eternal God, our refuge and strength, console and support those who are sorrowful through the comfort of your Word, so we might be confident in this and every time of need, trusting in your love, through Jesus Christ our Lord. Amen.

Or

Almighty God, whose love never fails, and who can turn the shadow of death into the light of life, illumine us through your Word; so that hearing your promises, we may be lifted out of darkness and distress into the light and peace of your presence, through Jesus Christ our Lord. Amen.

Lessons

There will ordinarily be two or three lessons, one from the Old Testament, one from a portion of the New Testament other than the Gospels, and one from the Gospels.

OLD TESTAMENT

Psalm 23	Psalm 84:1–4, 8–12
Psalm 27	Psalm 121
Psalm 42:11–43:5	

The reading may be followed by the Gloria Patri.

Glory be to the Father, and to the Son, and to the Holy Spirit: as it was in the beginning, is now, and ever shall be, world without end. Amen.

EPISTLE

Romans 8:28 (29–30), 31–35, 37–39	Philippians 2:1–11
1 Corinthians 15:49–57	Hebrews 12:18–24
2 Corinthians 4:5–18	Revelation 7:9–17

GOSPEL

Matthew 6:25–33	John 1:1–5, 9–14
Mark 5:22–42	John 6:25–40, 47–51
Luke 24:1–8, 36–43	John 14:1–6, 18, 19, 25–27

Sermon

A brief sermon may be preached. The focus of the sermon is the hope set before us in the gospel: that in life, in death, in life beyond death, God is with us. It may also be appropriate to acknowledge this hope as it was manifested in the life of the one who has died in the faith.

Ascription of Praise

Now to the one who is able to keep you from falling, to present you faultless before the presence of his glory with exceeding joy, to the only wise God our Savior, be glory and majesty, dominion and power, both now and for ever. Amen.

A hymn may be sung.

The Response to God

Confession of Faith

Let us confess our Christian faith using the Apostles' Creed.

> I believe in God, the Father almighty,
>   creator of heaven and earth.
>
> I believe in Jesus Christ, his only Son, our Lord.
>   He was conceived by the power of the Holy Spirit and
>   born of the Virgin Mary.
>   He suffered under Pontius Pilate,
>   was crucified, died, and was buried.

He descended to the dead.
On the third day he rose again.
He ascended into heaven
    and is seated at the right hand of the
    Father.
He will come again to judge the living and the dead.

I believe in the Holy Spirit,
    the holy catholic Church,
    the communion of saints,
    the forgiveness of sins,
    the resurrection of the body,
    and the life everlasting. Amen.

Or

I believe in God, the Father almighty,
    maker of heaven and earth;

And in Jesus Christ, his only Son, our Lord;
    who was conceived by the Holy Ghost,
    born of the Virgin Mary,
    suffered under Pontius Pilate,
    was crucified, dead, and buried.
    He descended into hell.
    The third day he rose again from the dead.
    He ascended into heaven,
    and sitteth on the right hand of God the Father almighty.
    From thence he shall come to judge the quick and the
        dead.

I believe in the Holy Ghost,
>the holy catholic Church,
>the communion of saints,
>the forgiveness of sins,
>the resurrection of the body,
>and the life everlasting. Amen.

N.B. A metrical version of the creed may be sung using the hymn "Rejoice in the Lord."

Or

"What then shall we say to this? If God is for us, who is against us? . . . Who shall separate us from the love of Christ? Shall tribulation, or distress, or persecution, or famine, or nakedness, or peril, or sword? . . . No, in all these things we are more than conquerors through him who loved us. For I am sure that neither death, nor life, nor angels, nor principalities, nor things present, nor things to come, nor powers, nor height, nor depth, nor anything else in all creation, will be able to separate us from the love of God in Christ Jesus our Lord" (Rom. 8:31, 35, 37–39 RSV).

Prayers of Thanksgiving and Intercession

Let us pray. O God, from the dawn of the first day you have cared for your people. By your hand we were created, in your hand we live, and to your hand we return again. You have revealed yourself in many and various ways, until, in the fullness of time, your word was made flesh and dwelt among us in the person of Jesus Christ our Lord. In his life, death, and resurrection we find our calling in this world and our hope for the world to come.

Therefore with your whole church on earth and with all the company of heaven we worship and adore your glorious name:

Holy, holy, holy, Lord, God of hosts. Heaven and earth are full of your glory. Hosanna in the highest! Blessed is he who comes in the name of the Lord. Hosanna in the highest!

O God, you understand our grief, for you have felt our pain. Jesus wept with Mary and Martha at the death of Lazarus, and the heavens were darkened when your own Son died upon the cross. Comfort us with the knowledge that Jesus raised his friend and will raise all who hear his voice, for he destroyed the darkness of death when you raised him to the light of Easter morn.

We give you thanks in this day for your servants, who, having lived this life in faith, now live eternally with you. Especially we thank you for _____, for the gift of his/her life, for the grace you have given him/her, for all in his/her life, for all in him/her that was good and kind and faithful. (*Here mention may be made of attributes or service.*) We thank you that for him/her death is past and pain is ended, and he/she has entered the joy you have prepared in the company of all the saints.

Give us faith to look beyond touch and sight, and in seeing that we are surrounded by so great a cloud of witnesses, enable us to run with perseverance the race that is set before us, looking to Jesus, the author and finisher of our faith. Bring us at last to your eternal peace, through Jesus Christ our Lord, in whose name we are bold to pray:

Our Father in heaven,
    hallowed be your name.
Your kingdom come.
Your will be done,
    on earth as it is in heaven.
Give us this day our daily bread.
And forgive us our debts,
    as we also have forgiven our debtors.
And do not bring us to the time of trial,
    but rescue us from the evil one.
For the kingdom and the power and the glory
    are yours forever. Amen. (NRSV)

Commendation

Into your hands, O merciful Savior, we commend your servant
_____. Acknowledge, we pray, a sheep of your fold, a lamb
of your own flock, a sinner of your own redeeming. Receive him/her
into the arms of your mercy, into the blessed rest of everlasting peace,
and into the glorious company of the saints in light. Let us go forth in
the name of Christ. Amen.

A hymn may be sung.

If the body is to be committed for burial, the service shall continue at the grave.

The Committal

Lessons

Psalm 121   Revelation 21:1–4
Revelation 14:13

Committal

As the body is committed to the grave, earth may be cast upon the coffin by the minister and/or the family and friends of the deceased.

We have entrusted our brother/sister _____ into the hands of God, and we now commit his/her body to the ground/deep/ elements/this resting place, earth to earth, ashes to ashes, dust to dust, in sure and certain hope of the resurrection to eternal life through our Lord Jesus Christ. The Lord bless him/her and keep him/her, the Lord make his face to shine upon him/her and be gracious unto him/ her, the Lord lift up his countenance upon him/her and grant him/ her peace. Amen.

Prayer

O God, in the beginning you formed us from the dust of the earth and breathed into us the breath of life. So also, in these last days, you have promised to raise us from the dust, so we might assume a new body at the coming of your Son. For as in Adam all die, so in Christ shall all be made alive. We thank you for this hope kindled within our hearts, that _____, who has died, will in the twinkling of an eye be raised to life imperishable.

Look down with tender pity and compassion upon us in this day, and grant unto each of us the comfort of your spirit. Renew within us the gifts of faith, hope, and love, through Jesus Christ our Lord, who lives and reigns with you and the Holy Spirit, world without end. Amen.

Benediction

Now the God of peace who brought again from the dead our Lord Jesus, the great shepherd of the sheep, by the blood of the eternal covenant, equip you with everything good that you may do his will, working in you that which is pleasing in his sight, through Jesus Christ; to whom be glory forever and ever. And the blessing of God almighty, Father, Son, and Holy Spirit, be and abide with you always. Amen.

James R. Esther and Donald J. Bruggink, eds., *Worship the Lord* (Grand Rapids: The Reformed Church in America, Eerdmans, 1987), 42–48. Used by permission.

PART 2

Special Situation Funeral and Memorial Services

12

On Occasion of Stillborn, Miscarriage, and Infant Deaths

Opening Words of Greeting

"As a father has compassion on his children, so the LORD has compassion on those who fear him; for he knows how we are formed, he remembers that we are dust.... But from everlasting to everlasting the LORD's love is with those who fear him, and his righteousness with their children's children" (Ps. 103:13–14, 17).

Dear friends, we have gathered here in our grief to draw on the strength the Lord provides and to witness to our faith in Christ who is the resurrection and the life. We acknowledge the human loss of _____, son/daughter of _____ and _____. A precious life was conceived. Sadly we accept this death. May the

Lord grant each of us grace, that in the midst of our pain we may find comfort, in our sorrow, hope, and in death, resurrection.

Pastoral Prayer

Almighty God, creator of life, whose ways are hidden from our finite, temporal sight, yet whose marvelous works are experienced every hour, our hearts go out to these parents in the loss and disappointment they feel with the premature death of one for whom they had yearned. It has come so shortly after birth/prior to birth. Bless now the mother who has carried this child lovingly. Bless also the father who sorrows here this day. You know the heaviness of heart. You share our griefs and sorrows. You know our broken dreams. You invite us to cast our burdens on you and find in your eternal arms the comfort and strength to go on.

Your Son, our Savior, has said, "Let the little children come to me, and do not hinder them; for the kingdom of God belongs to such as these." We commit to your loving arms this little life to dwell in your presence forever. Receive _____ into your loving arms. Receive us also that we may experience your healing in days to come. This we pray in the name of our resurrected, living Savior, even Jesus Christ the great shepherd of the sheep. Amen.

Scripture Reading

Select an appropriate reading(s) from this list.

Psalm 23

Isaiah 40:11

Isaiah 65:17–25

Jeremiah 31:15

Zechariah 8:1–8

Matthew 5:8

Matthew 18:1–5

Mark 10:13–16

John 14:1–3

2 Corinthians 1:3–4

Brief Meditation

As appropriate, this should include personal words of comfort and encouragement from Scripture. Pastors, friends, or family members may participate as requested by the grieving family.

Pastoral Prayer and the Lord's Prayer

Our Father in heaven,
hallowed be thy name,
your kingdom come;
your will be done,
on earth as it is in heaven.
Give us today our daily bread.
And forgive us our debts,
as we also have forgiven our debtors.
And lead us not into temptation,
but deliver us from the evil one.
For yours is the kingdom and the power and the glory forever. Amen.

Benediction

"May the God of peace, who through the blood of the eternal covenant brought back from the dead our Lord Jesus, that great Shepherd of the sheep, equip you with everything good for doing his will, and may he work in us what is pleasing to him, through Jesus Christ, to whom be glory for ever and ever. Amen" (Heb. 13:20–21).

"The peace of God, which transcends all understanding, will guard your hearts and your minds in Christ Jesus" (Phil. 4:7).

And the blessing of God almighty, Father, Son, and Holy Spirit, be among you and remain with you always. Amen.

13

Funeral for a Child

Option One

Musical Prelude

Introductory Words

We gather today to witness to our faith in the resurrected Christ, even while we mourn the death of _____, the child of _____ and _____. In our grief and loss, may we find comfort in the words of Scripture.

Jesus said: "Truly I tell you, unless you change and become like little children, you will never enter the kingdom of heaven. Therefore, whoever takes the lowly position of this child is the greatest in the kingdom of heaven. . . . See that you do not despise one of these little ones. For I tell you that their angels in heaven always see the face of my

Father in heaven. . . . In the same way your Father in heaven is not willing that any of these little ones should perish" (Matt. 18:3–4, 10, 14).

Jesus also said, "Let the little children come to me, and do not hinder them, for the kingdom of heaven belongs to such as these" (Matt. 19:14).

Prayer

Our heavenly Father, you were willing to give up your only beloved Son to face death on our behalf. You know the pain that comes in the loss of one dearly loved. Fill us with your grace to face this loss now of _____. We entrust him/her to your eternal arms, to enjoy the bliss of your eternal home and glorious presence forevermore. We recall the words of your Son who said, "Let the children come to me, for of such is the kingdom of heaven."

We pray that your love and peace might surround _____ (name members of family) and all the members of their family. Show compassion to them and comfort them this day and in the days that follow. May things unseen and that which is eternal grow more real to them and to all of us. May we long for that future promised resurrection when we who know Christ are united forever in your perfect heavenly kingdom. This we pray in the name of our living Savior who holds the keys to death and life. Amen.

Scripture Readings

Select from the following appropriate readings.

2 Samuel 12:16–23   Matthew 19:13–15

Psalm 103:6–18   Mark 10:13–16

Matthew 11:25–30   Revelation 7:17

Matthew 18:1–5, 10–14

Funeral Meditation

May be followed by personal comments by family members or friends of the family.

Hymn

"Children of the Heavenly Father"

"Jesus Loves Me"

"O God Our Help in Ages Past"

Prayer and Benediction

Most gracious Father, who in all the afflictions of your people are yourself afflicted, we commend to you the parents of this child. May you not leave them comfortless but give them assurance that all is well with _____. May the words of your Son, which remind us of your love and care for little children, breathe peace into their hearts this day. We pray this anticipating the blessed hope that one day they will be reunited with him/her in the joy of your eternal presence. This we pray in the words of Christ who taught us saying, Our Father . . .

"May the God of peace, who through the blood of the eternal covenant brought back from the dead our Lord Jesus, that great Shepherd of the sheep, equip you with everything good for doing his will, and may he work in us what is pleasing to him, through Jesus Christ, to whom be glory for ever and ever. Amen" (Heb. 13:20–21).

Option Two

Opening Words

Welcome

Invocation

We Express Our Emotions before God

Select one or more of the following readings and hymns.

Psalm of Praise—Psalm 100
Song—"Children of the Heavenly Father"

Psalm of Confidence—Psalm 23
Song—"Surely Goodness and Mercy" *or* "The Lord's My Shepherd"

Psalm of Grief—Psalm 77:1–9
Song—"I Cast All My Cares upon You"

Psalm of Thanksgiving—Psalm 121

Song—"To God Be the Glory" *or* "To the Hills I Lift My Eyes"

Sharing in God's Comfort

Words of Reflection

May include comments by relatives or friends of the family.

Prayer of Comfort

Song of Hope—"I've Got Peace Like a River" *or* "Standing on the Promises"

Closing Words of Comfort and Benediction

The God of peace, who brought again from the dead our Lord Jesus Christ, the great shepherd of the sheep, through the blood of the everlasting covenant, make you perfect in every good work to do his will, working in you that which is well-pleasing in his sight, through Jesus Christ, to whom be glory for ever and ever. Amen.

Closing Hymn—"Christ the Lord Is Risen Today"

14

Funeral for a Suicide or Other Tragic Circumstances

Prelude

Words of Introduction

We come today as a thirsty land crying out for rain, as a hungry heart longing for nourishment, as a lonely and frightened sheep pleading for rescue by the good shepherd, as that same sheep safe in the arms of the rescuer.

We hear the voice of our heavenly Father say, "Come to me, all you who are weary and burdened, and I will give you rest. Take my yoke upon you and learn from me, for I am gentle and humble in heart, and you will find rest for your souls" (Matt. 11:28–29).

Even though we are hurting and have unanswered questions, may "the peace of God, which transcends all understanding . . . guard your hearts and your minds in Christ Jesus" (Phil. 4:7). May the Father of compassion and the God of all comfort be with each of us as we now bow in prayer before him.

Prayer

With broken hearts and unanswered questions we come before you, our heavenly Father, to be healed, comforted, and strengthened. By your grace grant us forgiveness, mercy, and comfort. Hold us close to yourself. Help us to trust you. Help us sort through mixed-up and confused feelings so that we may face what we must in a triumphant way through our living Savior Jesus Christ.

We remember the one whom we have loved and who is now gone from our sight. We feel a profound loss. And so we turn to you, the eternal one, the resurrection and the life, to come among us this hour. Forgive our sins of omission and commission. Deal with us tenderly. May your peace, which transcends all understanding, guard the hearts and minds of family and friends as we rest in Christ Jesus, through whom we pray. Amen.

Or

Dear God, lover of your people, you hold dear all you have made. You understand our terrible fears, our deep depressions, our hopeless moments.

Our lives too are shattered by this terrible act. Gentle shepherd, lead us to peace, forgiveness, and hope. Deliver us from guilt and

bitterness, and heal our broken hearts. Help us to see beyond both
_____'s pain and our own to the wholesomeness of your king-
dom when we shall all gather in your presence and every tear will be
wiped away and every wrong made right, through Jesus Christ our
Lord. Amen.*

Hymn or Musical Selection

Old Testament Readings

2 Samuel 18:33	Psalm 55:22
Psalm 23	Psalm 130:1–2, 5–7
Psalm 27:1, 14	Psalm 139:1, 2, 7–12
Psalm 46:1, 2, 11	Isaiah 40:1, 28–31

New Testament Readings

Matthew 5:1–12	Hebrews 4:14–16
Romans 8:28, 35–39	1 John 4:7–13

Meditation

* Prayer from Leonard J. Vander Zee, ed., *In Life and In Death* (Grand Rapids: CRC
Publications, 1992), 202. All rights reserved. Used by permission.

Benediction

The Lord bless you and keep you; the Lord make his face shine upon you and be gracious to you; the Lord turn his face toward you and give you peace. In the name of the eternal and loving Father, Son, and Holy Spirit. Amen.

Postlude

15

Funeral for an Accident Victim

Prelude

"Holy Spirit, Truth Divine"

"Spirit of God, Descend upon My Heart"

"O Sacred Head, Now Wounded"

Opening Sentences

"Cast thy burden upon the LORD, and he shall sustain thee" (Ps. 55:22 KJV).

"He healeth the broken in heart, and bindeth up their wounds" (Ps. 147:3 KJV).

"Blessed are they that mourn: for they shall be comforted" (Matt. 5:4 KJV).

Invocation

With broken hearts and forlorn spirits, we come before you, O God, to be healed, comforted, and sustained. Dear Father, by your grace, grant us your forgiveness, mercy, and comfort. Enfold us within your fellowship of love and in the household of faith. Enlighten us in our seeking. Deepen us in our trusting. Unravel our mixed-up, confused feelings so that we may face what we must in a triumphant way, through Jesus Christ, the Lord. Amen.

Hymn

"Because He Lives"

"I Know That My Redeemer Lives"

Old Testament Scripture Readings

General Selections

Psalm 55:22   Isaiah 40:1, 28–31

Psalm 62:1–2

Specifically Relevant Selection

"The Lord is my light and my salvation; whom shall I fear? the Lord is the strength of my life; of whom shall I be afraid? . . . Wait on the Lord: be of good courage, and he shall strengthen thine heart: wait, I say, on the Lord" (Ps. 27:1, 14 KJV).

New Testament Scripture Readings

General Selection

Romans 8:35–39

Specifically Relevant Selection

"And we know that all things work together for good to them that love God, to them who are the called according to his purpose" (Rom. 8:28 KJV).

Pastoral Prayer

God, you have so mysteriously made us that so living in this temporal house we still may think your thoughts. We are but children of a day— our sun has its rising and its setting; yet deep within us we know the instinct of immortality and reach for eternity.

We thank you, dear God, for the gift of memory and for the ties that bind our hearts in love. We remember just now the one we have long loved and admired, who is now gone from our sight. His/her name is precious in our memory. His/her life was dear to our hearts. We feel a profound loss. Dear Lord, join to our company today his/ her invisible presence, help us to believe in your infinite world where he/she is still alive, so that barren places may rejoice and the desert of our hearts may blossom again.

We thank you for the life of Jesus, giving visible expression to what we yearn for and to the quality of your being. Merciful Father, forgive our contradictions, our neglect, our selfishness. Forgive what we have done that we should not have done, and the things we have left undone that we should have done. Lord, help us inculcate Jesus into our heart that we may share his abundant life, his resurrection, and his peace, which the world cannot take away. So may it be. Amen.

Hymn

"There Is No Sorrow, Lord, Too Light" (stanzas 1–3)

Meditation

Benediction

May almighty God, the Father, the Son, and the Holy Spirit, bless you and keep you, now and forever. Amen.

Postlude

"O Love That Will Not Let Me Go"
"Lead, Kindly Light"
"Abide with Me"

James L. Christensen, *Difficult Funeral Services* (Grand Rapids: Revell, 1985), 68–73. Used by permission.

16

Funeral for an Unbeliever

Prelude

Opening Words

"The eternal God is thy refuge, and underneath are the everlasting arms" (Deut. 33:27 KJV).

"The LORD is nigh unto them that are of a broken heart; and saveth such as be of a contrite spirit" (Ps. 34:18 KJV).

"He healeth the broken in heart, and bindeth up their wounds.... Great is our Lord, and of great power: his understanding is infinite" (Ps. 147:3, 5 KJV).

"The secret things belong unto the LORD our God: but those things which are revealed belong unto us ... for ever" (Deut. 29:29 KJV).

Invocation

Eternal God, you know all things in earth and heaven, you are our refuge and strength and our help in times of trouble. Fill our hearts with trust in you so we might receive comfort and find your grace to help us in this time of need and loss in the death of _____. We trust in your care and providence through Jesus Christ our Lord. Amen.

Scripture Reading

> Psalm 24:3–5
> Psalm 89:1–2, 5–15, 32
> Psalm 119:129–35
> Psalm 142:5–7
> Ecclesiastes 3:1–8
> Romans 10:9–13
> Philippians 4:6–13

Meditation

Funerals are for the living rather than for the dead. In the case of one who does not profess to be a Christian, the minister should avoid the extreme of condemning the deceased to eternal punishment or preaching the deceased into heaven. He must avoid judging the heart as well as giving false hope. The good news of the gospel can be carefully presented without saying that the promised blessings necessarily apply to the deceased. *The following are some ideas for developing into a meditation.*

Meditate on the character of God as revealed in Psalm 89:1–2. The psalmist had a difficult time understanding what the Lord was doing, yet he knew God better than to doubt his goodness. Scripture asks, "Shall not the Judge of all the earth do right?" (Gen. 18:25 KJV). God is too good to be unkind and too wise to make mistakes. He is always trustworthy.

Whenever we are perplexed, we can certainly trust the Lord to do what is right. Righteousness and justice are his foundations. Reliability and faithfulness continue to be his attributes. By meditating on his righteous goodness and faithfulness, we can put aside our fears and doubts. We can keep on trusting him whatever the storms in life.

While we can't do anything now for the dead, we can minister to the needs of the living. We can look for opportunities to share the good news of salvation to all who turn to Christ.

Prayer

Lord God almighty, we gather in this service united in prayer with the family of _____. You have taught us that you are the righteous and faithful creator of all. We ask that you comfort each relative and friend here today by reminding them that, even as they now mourn, they can be grateful for the one whose life was such that, when he/she is gone, there is a vacuum. We acknowledge that he/she will be missed.

You as the omniscient one are the only one able to search our hearts and know us perfectly. We commend _____ to your merciful care, knowing that as judge of all the earth, you will do what is right.

Comfort us who are yet living. Teach us to number our days that we may grow in wisdom and in faith. May this encourage all of us left behind to prepare for eternal life that comes through your Son Jesus Christ, who died and rose again, that we might have life everlasting. It's in his name that we now pray and receive his comfort. Amen.

Hymn or Special Music

Benediction

May God be merciful to us and bless us. May he cause his face to shine upon us. May the grace of our Lord Jesus Christ, and the love of God the Father, and the fellowship of the Holy Spirit, be with you all, both now, and on into eternity. Amen.

PART 3

Graveside and Committal Services

17

Supplemental Committal Services

Option One

Services of committal are included with some of the denominational services in part 1. The following are supplemental committal services.

Scripture

"I am the resurrection, and the life," saith the Lord: "he that believeth in me, though he were dead, yet shall ye live: and whosoever liveth and believeth in me shall never die" (John 11:25–26 KJV).

"For we know that if our earthly house of this tabernacle were dissolved, we have a building of God, a house not made with hands, eternal in the heavens" (2 Cor. 5:1 KJV).

"Fear not; I am the first and the last, saith the Lord: I am he that liveth, and was dead; and, behold, I am alive for evermore" (Rev. 1:17–18 KJV).

"Thou wilt keep him in perfect peace, whose mind is stayed on thee: because he trusteth in thee" (Isa. 26:3 KJV).

"Lord, to whom shall we go? Thou hast the words of eternal life" (John 6:68 KJV).

Thanks be unto God who giveth us the victory.

Words of Committal

Unto the mercy of almighty God, we commend the soul of our departed brother/sister, and we commit his/her body to the ground, earth to earth, ashes to ashes, dust to dust, in the sure and certain hope of the resurrection to eternal life, through Jesus Christ our Lord. Amen.

"Blessed are the dead which die in the Lord from henceforth: Yea, saith the Spirit, that they may rest from their labours; and their works do follow them" (Rev. 14:13 KJV).

Prayer

O Lord, support us all the day long, until the shadows lengthen, and the evening comes, and the busy world is hushed, and the fever of life is over, and our work is done. Then, in thy mercy, grant us a safe lodging, and a holy rest, and peace at the last, through Jesus Christ our Lord. Amen.

Or

Almighty God, who by the death of thy dear Son Jesus Christ hast destroyed death, by his rest in the tomb hast sanctified the graves of the saints, and by his glorious resurrection hast brought life and immortality to light: receive, we beseech thee, our unfeigned thanks for that victory over death and the grave that he hath obtained for us and for all who sleep in him. Keep us in everlasting fellowship with all who wait for thee on earth, and with all who are with thee in heaven, in union with him who is the resurrection and the life, who liveth and reigneth with thee and the Holy Spirit, ever one God, world without end. Amen.

The Lord's Prayer

Benediction

The peace of God, which passeth all understanding, keep your hearts and minds in the knowledge and love of God, and of his Son Jesus Christ our Lord; and the blessing of God almighty, the Father, the Son, and the Holy Spirit, be upon you, and remain with you always. Amen.

The Book of Common Worship (Philadelphia: The Board of Christian Education of the Presbyterian Church in the United States of America, 1946), 213–15. Used by permission of Westminster John Knox.

Option Two

Words of Scripture

John 11:25–26

1 Corinthians 15:51, 53–57

2 Corinthians 5:1

1 Thessalonians 4:13–18

Revelation 21:1–7

Words of Committal

In sure and certain hope of the resurrection to eternal life promised through our Lord Jesus Christ, we commit to God almighty our brother/sister _____. We commit his/her body to the ground, earth to earth, ashes to ashes, dust to dust. We also commit his/her spirit to the loving care of the everlasting God, in anticipation of the future resurrection into life eternal. We believe the promise of Christ that he is the resurrection and the life, and all who believe in him, though they die, yet shall live. Even so come, Lord Jesus. Amen.

Option for cremation service.

In sure and certain hope of the resurrection to eternal life promised through our Lord Jesus Christ, we commit the remains of _____ to this prepared resting place so that ashes may return to ashes, and dust to dust. We commit the imperishable spirit to be forever with the Lord God almighty. We believe the promise of Christ that he is the resurrection and the life, and all who believe in him, though they die, yet shall live. Even so come, Lord Jesus. Amen.

Prayer

Father of all mercies and God of all comfort, we call on you in the name of our Lord and Savior Jesus Christ who is the resurrection and the life, who holds the keys to life and death. We pray for those who mourn this day, that in casting all their cares on you they may experience your care for them. Uphold them as they believe in the good news of life beyond the grave, of a future resurrection unto life eternal, of a future reunion with all who have died in Christ. Enable us to see beyond this place and time to your eternal kingdom. Prepare us all for that heavenly kingdom where every tear will be wiped away, death and sickness will be no more, and we will enjoy your presence forevermore. We pray all this through the name of Jesus Christ who is with us and remains the same yesterday, today, and forever. Amen.

The Lord's Prayer may follow.

Affirmation of Faith (optional)

Apostles' Creed

Or

We believe there is no condemnation for those who are in Christ Jesus; and we know that in everything God works for good with those who love him, who are called according to his purpose. We are sure that neither death, nor life, nor angels, nor principalities, nor things present, nor things to come, nor powers, nor height, nor depth, nor anything else in all creation, will be able to separate us from the love of God in Christ Jesus our Lord. Amen.

Or

This is the good news that we have received, in which we stand and by which we are saved, if we hold it fast: that Christ died for our sins according to the Scriptures, that he was buried, that he was raised on the third day, and that he appeared first to the women, then to Peter, and to the Twelve, and then to many faithful witnesses. We believe that Jesus is the Christ, the Son of the living God. Jesus Christ is the first and the last, the beginning and the end; he is our Lord and our God. We believe that the Lord himself shall descend from heaven with a shout, with the voice of the archangel, and with the trump of God: and the dead in Christ shall rise first. Then we who are alive and remain shall be caught up together with them in the clouds, to meet the Lord in the air. And so shall we ever be with the Lord. Amen.

Benediction

The Lord bless you and keep you. The Lord make his face shine upon you, and be gracious unto you. The Lord lift up his countenance upon you, and give you peace. In the name of the Father, the resurrected Son, and Holy Spirit. Amen.

Military Honors (optional)

If a military honor guard is present, it is customary for this unit to remove the flag from the casket, fold it, and present it to a member of the family.

18

Service of Interment
or Scattering of Ashes

In the case of cremation, some families prefer to have a memorial service in the church or funeral home. Afterward they may have a service of interment at the grave site at which a graveside committal service is used. Others who prefer not to bury an urn containing ashes may choose not to have an additional service. Instead they may prefer a private interment or scattering of ashes. In the latter case, the following service may be used.

Welcome

Welcome to this gathering of remembrance and farewell to _____.
We come acknowledging that this life is temporary and transitory. Dust we are and to dust we return. But we gather in hope—hope based on the resurrection of Jesus Christ who promised a future resurrection to

all who trust in Christ for salvation. The Lord has prepared a heavenly dwelling place. Let's take comfort now in the living words of Scripture.

Scripture Reading

I am convinced, says the apostle Paul, that neither death nor life, neither angels nor demons, neither the present nor the future, nor any powers, neither height nor depth, nor anything else in all creation, will be able to separate us from the love of God that is in Christ Jesus our Lord. (Rom. 8:38–39)

I lift up my eyes to the mountains—
    where does my help come from?
My help comes from the LORD,
    the Maker of heaven and earth.

He will not let your foot slip—
    he who watches over you will not slumber;
indeed, he who watches over Israel
    will neither slumber nor sleep.

The LORD watches over you—
    the LORD is your shade at your right hand;
the sun will not harm you by day,
    nor the moon by night.

The LORD will keep you from all harm—
    he will watch over your life;
the LORD will watch over your coming and going
    both now and forevermore. (Ps. 121)

Praise be to the God and Father of our Lord Jesus Christ! In his great mercy he has given us new birth into a living hope through the resurrection of Jesus Christ from the dead, and into an inheritance that can never perish, spoil or fade. This inheritance is kept in heaven for you, who through faith are shielded by God's power until the coming of the salvation that is ready to be revealed in the last time. (1 Pet. 1:3–5)

Prayer of Committal

Almighty God, our heavenly Father, we now praise you for the sure and certain hope of the resurrection to eternal life for everyone who dies trusting in the Lord Jesus Christ for salvation. We now commit the ashes of _____ to the ground/sea, earth to earth, ashes to ashes, dust to dust, rejoicing that on the last day Christ has promised to transform the bodies of all who trust in him into the likeness of his own glorious resurrection body. Amen.

Prayer for Family and Friends

Almighty God, Father of all mercies and giver of all comfort, deal graciously and kindly, we pray, with those who mourn, and especially with the family and friends of _____ gathered here, so that casting all their cares on you, each may know and experience the comfort of your love and presence through Jesus Christ our Lord. Amen.

Benediction

Now may the grace of our Lord Jesus Christ, and the love of God the Father, and the fellowship of the Holy Spirit, be with us all forever. Amen.

PART 4

Resources

19

Ministry to the Dying

What is your only comfort in life and in death?

That I am not my own, but belong—body and soul, in life and in death—to my faithful Savior Jesus Christ. He has fully paid for all my sins with his precious blood, and has set me free from the tyranny of the devil. He also watches over me in such a way that not a hair can fall from my head without the will of my Father in heaven: in fact, all things must work together for my salvation. Because I belong to him, Christ, by his Holy Spirit, assures me of eternal life and makes me wholeheartedly willing and ready from now on to live for him (*Heidelberg Catechism* Q & A 1).

Scriptures

Psalm 16:8–11	John 14:1–3
Psalm 23	Romans 8:35, 37–39
Psalm 91	1 Corinthians 15:50, 53–57
Psalm 103:1, 8, 10–14	2 Corinthians 1:3–11
Psalm 121	2 Corinthians 4:16–5:1
Luke 23:33, 39–43	Revelation 1:17–18
John 11:25–27	Revelation 21:1–4

Prayers

With Those Who Are Unable to Communicate

Our heavenly Father, you are the all-knowing one. You knew us before our birth and throughout our lifetime, and you will continue to love us for all eternity. We pray that your loving presence and sustaining grace will be real in _____'s life. Assure him/her that nothing can separate us from your love. May he/she rest in your loving arms and feel your shepherding care. This we pray in the name of our resurrected Savior, Jesus Christ. Amen.

With Those Who Have Alzheimer's Disease

Lord God, we pray to you through the name of Jesus Christ who is the same yesterday, today, and forever. He has borne our sorrows and carried our griefs. Guard the heart and mind of _____ with your perfect peace that surpasses human understanding. Although the pain of his/her forgetfulness is great, we rejoice that you continue to remember him/her in your loving care. May you now provide for each of his/her needs according to your riches in glory through Jesus Christ. For it's in his name that we pray. Amen.

With Those Suffering from AIDS

Father of mercy, and God of all compassion, you are totally aware of what we need even before we ask it. You understand our deepest worries and fears. May you now calm those worries and fears as _____ places trust in Jesus Christ. Help him/her to rely and draw upon your strength. Grant wisdom and compassion to doctors and nurses who care for him/her. Grant his/her family comfort and the assurance of your shepherding care. This we pray in the name of Jesus Christ, who died and rose again on our behalf. Amen.

When Life Support Systems Are Withdrawn

Our compassionate and loving Lord, you have breathed into us the breath of life. You have given us the opportunity to exercise our minds and our wills. In our weakness and frailty, we surrender all life to you, our creator, trusting in your gracious promises. This we pray through Jesus Christ who is now here with us. Amen.

For Someone Dying

Lord God, you are the Alpha and the Omega, the beginning and the end. You hold in your hands the keys of life and death. You remain with us and continue to love us in life and in death. Help _____ now to trust in your goodness and to claim your promise of life everlasting through Jesus Christ who died for our sins and was raised for our justification. Cleanse him/her of all sin and remove all burdens. May you in your perfect timing welcome him/her into your loving arms in your peaceful, heavenly kingdom. May the grace of our Lord Jesus Christ, and the love of God the Father, and the fellowship of the Holy Spirit be with him/her now and on into eternity. Amen.

20

Scripture Readings
and Confessions of Faith

Scripture Readings

Old Testament

2 Samuel 12:18–24

Job 8:9

Job 9:23–26

Job 19:25–27

Proverbs 31:10–31

Ecclesiastes 3:1–15

Ecclesiastes 5:15

Ecclesiastes 12:1–8

Isaiah 26:1–4, 12, 16–17, 19

Isaiah 35:3–10

Isaiah 40:1–11, 28–31

Isaiah 43:1–3, 5–7

Isaiah 65:17–25

Lamentations 3:1–9, 17–26

Zechariah 8:1–8

Psalms

Psalm 1	Psalm 90
Psalm 16:1–2, 5–11	Psalm 91
Psalm 22:1–5, 19, 22–24	Psalm 103
Psalm 23	Psalm 116
Psalm 25:1–7, 10, 14–18, 20–22	Psalm 121
	Psalm 130
Psalm 27:1–13	Psalm 131
Psalm 39	Psalm 139
Psalm 46	Psalm 146
Psalm 62	

Gospels

Matthew 5:1–12	Luke 23:33, 39–46, 52–53
Matthew 11:25–30	Luke 24:1–6
Matthew 18:1–5, 10	John 5:19–29
Matthew 25:31–46	John 6:37–40
Matthew 28:1–15	John 11:21–27, 32–45
Mark 10:13–16	John 12:23–26
Mark 16:1–13	John 14:1–6
Luke 7:11–17	

Epistles

Acts 10:34–43

Romans 2:12–26

Romans 5:1–11

Romans 8:14–23, 31–35,
37–39

Romans 14:7–9, 10–12

1 Corinthians 2:9

1 Corinthians 15:20–28,
51–58

2 Corinthians 4:7–18

2 Corinthians 5:1–10

Philippians 1:29

Philippians 3:10

Philippians 3:20–21

Colossians 2:9–12

1 Thessalonians 4:13–18

2 Timothy 2:8–13

2 Timothy 4:6–8

Hebrews 9:27

Hebrews 11:1–3, 6–7, 12–16

Hebrews 12:1–2

James 4:13–15

1 Peter 1:3–9

1 John 3:1–3

Revelation 1:18

Revelation 7:9–17

Revelation 14:1–3, 6–7, 12–13

Revelation 20:11–21:1

Revelation 21:1–5, 6–7

Confessions of Faith

The Apostles' Creed

I believe in God, the Father almighty, creator of heaven and earth.
I believe in Jesus Christ, his only Son, our Lord. He was conceived by
the power of the Holy Spirit, and born of the Virgin Mary. He suffered
under Pontius Pilate, was crucified, died, and was buried; he descended
to hell. On the third day he rose again. He ascended into heaven, and

is seated at the right hand of the Father. He will come again to judge the living and the dead.

I believe in the Holy Spirit, the holy catholic Church, the communion of saints, the forgiveness of sin, the resurrection of the body, and the life everlasting. Amen.

The Nicene Creed

We believe in one God, the Father, the Almighty, maker of heaven and earth, of all that is, seen and unseen.

We believe in one Lord, Jesus Christ, the only Son of God, eternally begotten of the Father, God from God, Light from Light, true God from true God, begotten, not made, of one Being with the Father. Through him all things were made. For us men and for our salvation he came down from heaven: by the power of the Holy Spirit he became incarnate from the Virgin Mary, and was made man. For our sake he was crucified under Pontius Pilate; he suffered death and was buried. On the third day he rose again in accordance with the Scriptures; he ascended into heaven and is seated at the right hand of the Father. He will come again in glory to judge the living and the dead, and his kingdom will have no end.

We believe in the Holy Spirit, the Lord, the giver of life, who proceeds from the Father (and the Son). With the Father and the Son he is worshiped and glorified. He has spoken through the Prophets. We believe in one holy catholic and apostolic Church. We acknowledge one baptism. We look for the resurrection of the dead, and the life of the world to come. Amen.

Heidelberg Catechism

QUESTION AND ANSWER 1

What is your only comfort in life and in death?

That I am not my own, but belong—body and soul, in life and in death—to my faithful Savior Jesus Christ. He has fully paid for all my sins with his precious blood, and has set me free from the tyranny of the devil. He also watches over me in such a way that not a hair can fall from my head without the will of my Father in heaven: in fact, all things must work together for my salvation. Because I belong to him, Christ, by his Holy Spirit, assures me of eternal life and makes me wholeheartedly willing and ready from now on to live for him.

QUESTION AND ANSWER 45

How does Christ's resurrection benefit us?

First, by his resurrection he has overcome death, so that he might make us share in the righteousness he won for us by his death.

Second, by his power we too are already now resurrected to a new life.

Third, Christ's resurrection is a guarantee of our glorious resurrection.

QUESTION AND ANSWER 57

How does "the resurrection of the body" comfort you?

Not only my soul will be taken immediately after this life to Christ its head, but even my very flesh, raised by the power of Christ, will be reunited with my soul and made like Christ's glorious body.

QUESTION AND ANSWER 58

How does the article concerning "life everlasting" comfort you?

Even as I already now experience in my heart the beginning of eternal joy, so after this life I will have perfect blessedness such as no eye has seen, no ear has heard, no human heart has ever imagined: a blessedness in which to praise God eternally.

Westminster Shorter Catechism

QUESTION AND ANSWER 37

What benefits do believers receive from Christ when they die?

When believers die, their souls are made perfectly holy and immediately pass into glory. Their bodies, which are still united to Christ, rest in the grave until the resurrection.

QUESTION AND ANSWER 38

What benefits do believers receive from Christ at the resurrection?

At the resurrection, believers, raised in glory, will be publicly recognized and declared not guilty on the day of judgment and will be made completely happy in the full enjoyment of God forever.

New Testament Confession #1

We believe there is no condemnation for those who are in Christ Jesus: and we know that in everything God works for good with those who love him, who are called according to his purpose. We are sure that neither death, nor life, nor angels, nor principalities, nor things present, nor things to come, nor powers, nor height, nor depth, nor anything else in all creation, will be able to separate us from the love of God in Christ Jesus our Lord. Amen.

New Testament Confession #2

This is the good news that we have received, in which we stand, and by which we are saved, if we hold it fast: that Christ died for our sins according to the Scriptures, that he was buried, that he was raised on the third day, and that he appeared first to the women, then to Peter, and to the Twelve, and then to many faithful witnesses. We believe that Jesus is the Christ, the Son of the living God. Jesus Christ is the first and the last, the beginning and the end; he is our Lord and our God. Amen.

New Testament Confession #3

We believe that Jesus Christ is the Son of God, that God has given to us eternal life and this life is in his Son; that he is the resurrection and the life, and that whoever believes on him, though he were dead, yet shall he live.

We believe that if we confess our sins, he is faithful and just to forgive us our sins and to cleanse us from all unrighteousness. We believe that the world passes away and the lust thereof, but he who does the will of God abides forever.

21

Hymns for Funerals and Memorial Services

"Abide with Me"

"All Must Be Well"

"All Things New"

"Be Still My Soul"

"By the Sea of Crystal"

"Children of the Heavenly Father"

"Christ, the Life of All the Living"

"Christ the Lord Is Risen Today"

"Face to Face"

"For All the Saints"

"God Moves in a Mysterious Way"

"Great Is Thy Faithfulness"

"Guide Me, O My Great Redeemer"

"Holy God, We Praise Your Name"

"How Firm a Foundation"

"How Great Thou Art"

"I Greet My Sure Redeemer"

"It Is Not Death to Die"

"It Is Well with My Soul"

"Jerusalem the Golden"

"Jesus Lives and So Do We"

"Jesus, Lover of My Soul"

"Jesus, Savior, Pilot Me"

"Jesus Shall Reign"

"Lo! He Comes with Clouds Descending"

"My Faith Looks Up to Thee"

"My Jesus, I Love Thee"

"Nearer, My God to Thee"

"Near to the Heart of God"

"O Father, You Are Sovereign"

"O God, Our Help in Ages Past"

"O Love of God, How Strong and True"

"O Love That Wilt Not Let Me Go"

"Out of the Depths"

"Praise, My Soul, the King of Heaven"

"Precious Lord, Take My Hand"

"Rock of Ages"

"Sing Praise to God Who Reigns Above"

"Still, My Soul, Be Still"

"Swing Low, Sweet Chariot"

"Ten Thousand Times Ten Thousand"

"The God of Abraham Praise"

"The King Shall Come When Morning Dawns"

"The Lord's My Shepherd"

"The Perfect Wisdom of Our God"

"There Is a Hope"

"Thine Is the Glory"

"Under His Wings"

"What a Friend We Have in Jesus"

22

Quotations, Illustrations, and Last Words

Quotations for Use in Funeral Messages

Denial and Fear of Death

We consider ourselves immortal, or at least as though [we are] going to live for centuries. Folly of the human spirit! Every day those who die soon follow those who are already dead. One about to leave on a journey ought not to think himself far from one who went only two days before. Life flows by like a flood.

François Fénelon, *Christian Perfection*

It will only be sad for those who have not thought about it.

François Fénelon, *Christian Perfection*

The health of our bodies, the passions of our minds, the noise and hurry and pleasures and business of the world, lead us on with eyes that see not and ears that hear not.

William Law, *A Serious Call to a Devout and Holy Life*

Keeping Death in Our Thoughts

Thou oughtest so to order thyself in all thy thoughts and actions, as if today thou wert about to die.

Thomas à Kempis, *Imitation of Christ*

Labor now to live so, that at the hour of death thou mayest rather rejoice than fear. . . . Happy is he that always hath the hour of his death before his eyes, and daily prepareth himself to die. . . . When it is morning, think thou mayest die before night, and when evening comes, dare not to promise thyself the next morning. Be thou therefore always in a readiness, and so lead thy life that death may never take thee unprepared.

Thomas à Kempis, *Imitation of Christ*

The Christian's view of death is different from that of the great unbelieving mass of people in the world. Christians look at it as a journey and departure out of this misery and vale of tears (where the devil is prince and god) into yonder life, where there will be inexpressible and glorious joy and eternal blessedness. Diligently they study the art of looking at death in this way. Daily they practice it, and earnestly they ask our dear Lord Christ to grant them a blessed hour of departure and to comfort them in it with His Spirit, that they may commit their soul to Him with true faith, understanding, and confession. To such people death is not terrible but sincerely welcome.

Ascribed to Martin Luther

Wise shoppers clip coupons. Wise Christians clip obituaries.

Gary Thomas, *Seeking the Face of God*
(Eugene, OR: Harvest House, 1999), 156

You cannot pass a day devoutly unless you think of it as your last. The thought of death is the most essential of all works. The man who lives daily with the thought of death is to be admired, and the man who gives himself to it by the hour is surely a saint.

John Climacus, *The Ladder of Divine Ascent*

Changed Perspective When We Think of Death

A man who has heard himself sentenced to death will not worry about the way theatres are run.

John Climacus, *The Ladder of Divine Ascent*

I think we have lost the old knowledge that happiness is overrated—that, in a way, life is overrated. We have lost somehow a sense of mystery—about us, our purpose, our meaning, our role. Our ancestors believed in two worlds, and understood this to be the solitary, poor, nasty, brutish and short one. We are the first generation of man that actually expected to find happiness here on earth, and our search for it has caused such unhappiness. The reason: if you do not believe in another, higher world, if you believe only in the flat material world around you, if you believe that this is your only chance at happiness—if that is what you believe, then you are more than disappointed when the world does not give you a good measure of its riches, you are in despair.

Peggy Noonan, "You'd Cry Too if It Happened to You,"
Forbes 150 (1992)

He cannot die badly who lives well; and scarcely shall he die well who lives badly.

St. Augustine

The worst thing that can happen to you is not the death of a loved one, a prolonged illness, or a painful accident. The worst thing that could happen to you would be to suffer *for nothing*, die, and be lost forever. God's people suffer for something—for Someone—and when they die, they enter into heaven where all their investment of suffering is transformed into glory.

Warren W. Wiersbe, *Looking Up When Life Gets You
Down* (Grand Rapids: Baker Books, 2012), 156

O then, as you expect peace or rest in the chamber of death, get union with Christ. A grace with Christ is a comfortable place.

John Flavel, *Whole Works of the Rev. Mr. John Flavel*, vol. 5

Remembering Death Controls Our Passions

To render passion harmless let us behave as though we had only a week to live.

Thomas à Kempis, *Imitation of Christ*

The best way for anyone to know how much he ought to aspire after holiness is to consider not how much will make his present life easy, but to ask himself how much he thinks will make him easy at the hour of death.

William Law, *A Serious Call to a Devout and Holy Life*

Remembering Death Stimulates Spiritual Growth

Didst thou oftener think of thy death than of thy living long, there is no question but thou wouldst be more zealous to improve it. If also thou didst but consider within thyself the infernal pains in the other world, I believe thou wouldst willingly undergo any labor or sorrow in this world, and not be afraid of the greatest austerity. But because these things enter not to the heart, and we still love those things only that delight us, therefore we remain cold and very dull in religion.

Thomas à Kempis, *Imitation of Christ*

As of all foods, bread is the most essential, so the thought of death is the most necessary of all works. The remembrance of death amongst those in the midst of society gives birth to distress and meditation, and even more, to despondency. But amongst those who are free from noise, it produces the putting aside of cares and constant prayer and guarding of the mind. . . . He who with undoubting trust daily expects death is virtuous; but he who hourly yields himself to it is a saint.

John Climacus, *The Ladder of Divine Ascent*

Keeping Proper Perspective on Death

Feasts and business and pleasures and enjoyments seem great things to us whilst we think of nothing else; but as soon as we add death to them, they all sink into an equal littleness; and the soul that is separated from the body no more laments the loss of business than the losing of a feast.

William Law, *A Serious Call to a Devout and Holy Life*

The grave is not a period at the end of the sentence of life, but a conjunction connecting us with the life to come.

Larry Briney, *Daily Grace for the Daily Grind*
(n.p.: Xulon Press, 2004), 296

While others talked about what they would do if they heard that they had to die within that very hour, Saint Charles Borromaeus said he would continue his game of chess. For he had begun it only in honor of God, and he could wish for nothing better than to be called away in the midst of an action undertaken in the honor of God.

Frederick William Faber, *The Life and
Letters of Frederick William Faber*

Death wounds us, but wounds are meant to heal. And—given time—they will. But we must want to be healed. We cannot be like the child who keeps picking the scab from a cut. Life must move forward, even though we may have lost the one who was the dearest to us, even though meaning seems to have been removed from living.

Joseph Bayly, *The View from a Hearse*
(Colorado Springs: David C. Cook, 1969), 1973

What shall I say? A holy and good God has covered us with a dark cloud. O that we may kiss the rod, and lay our hands on our mouths! The Lord has done it.

> Sarah Edwards, letter of April 3, 1758, to her daughter
> Esther on the death of her husband, Jonathan Edwards

Illustrations for Use at Funerals

- General William Nelson was a Union general in the Civil War. He was shot and wounded mortally in the chest in Kentucky. As his men ran up the stairs he spoke just one phrase, "Send for a clergyman: I wish to be baptized." He had never taken the time during his youth or his early career to prepare for death. And now that he was wounded, it didn't stop the war. Everything was unchanged except the general's priorities. With mere minutes left before going into eternity, he finally cared for only one thing: preparing for eternity. He wanted to be baptized. Minutes later he died.

- At the funeral of former Soviet leader Leonid Brezhnev, his widow carried out a silent protest. She stood motionless by the coffin until seconds before the lid was closed on her husband's body. Then, just before the soldiers lowered the lid, Brezhnev's wife performed an act of great hope and courage. She reached down and made the sign of the cross on her husband's chest. Standing in that citadel of atheistic power, the wife of the man who had run it all hoped that her husband was wrong in his atheistic Communism. She hoped there was another life for her husband beyond this one. She hoped that the Jesus who died on the cross and arose might have mercy on her husband at his death.

• An Indiana cemetery has an old tombstone that bears this epitaph: "Pause, Stranger, when you pass me by. As you are now, so once was I. As I am now, so you will be. So prepare for death and follow me." A passerby once read those words and scratched his reply below: "To follow you I'm not content, until I know which way you went." He was right. The important thing about death is what follows.

• Billy Graham, at the funeral of Richard Nixon, related the story of how Winston Churchill planned his own funeral with the hope of the resurrection in mind. Churchill instructed that after the benediction a bugler, positioned high in the dome of St. Paul's Cathedral, play "Taps"—the universal signal indicating that the day is over. But then came the most dramatic part. Churchill instructed that another bugler, on the other side of the dome, play the notes of "Reveille"—the universal signal that a new day has dawned and it's time to arise. So Churchill was testifying that at the end of history the last note will not be "Taps" but "Reveille." There is hope beyond the grave because Christ has opened to us the door to heaven and new life by his own death and resurrection.

• The story is told of what Donald Grey Barnhouse, Presbyterian minister and author, said to his children while driving them in the car to the funeral of their mother. A large tractor trailer truck crossed in front of their car at an intersection, casting a fleeting shadow on their car. Dr. Barnhouse asked his children, "Would you rather be struck by the truck or the shadow?" The children predictably answered, "The shadow, of course." Barnhouse replied, "That's what has happened to us. Mother's dying is only the shadow of death. The lost sinner is struck by the tractor-trailer of death."

• When John Wesley was asked what he would do if he knew he were to die that night, he said that he would eat his supper, preach at the candlelight service, say his prayers, and go to bed. The monument to John and Charles Wesley in Westminster Abbey in London reads, "God buries his workmen, but carries on his work."

• The famous evangelist Dwight L. Moody once said that someday people would read that D. L. Moody of East Northfield had died. "Don't believe a word of it," he said, "because at that moment I shall be more alive than I am now. I was born of the flesh in 1837. I was born of the spirit in 1856. That which is born of flesh may die. That which is born of the spirit will live forever."

Last Words of the Dying

John Quincy Adams (1767–1848)
"It is the last of earth, I am content."

Richard Baxter (1615–91)
"I have pain, but I have peace, I have peace."

Thomas Becket (1117–70)
"For the name of Jesus and the defense of the church I am willing to die."

Henry Ward Beecher (1813–87)
"Now comes the mystery."

Ludwig van Beethoven (1770–1827)

"I shall hear in Heaven."

John Bradford (1510–55)

To a fellow martyr: "Be of good comfort, brother, for we shall have a merry supper with the Lord this night."

David Brainerd (1718–57)

"Lord, now let thy servant depart in peace."

Robert Bruce (1554–1631)

"Now God be with you, my dear children: I have breakfasted with you, and I shall sup with my Lord Jesus Christ."

John Bunyan (1628–88)

"Weep not for me, but for yourselves. I go to the Father of our Lord Jesus Christ, who will no doubt receive me. . . . I hope we shall ere long meet to sing the new song and remain happy forever, world without end. Amen."

John Calvin (1509–64)

"Thou, Lord, bruisest me; but I am abundantly satisfied, since it is from thy hand."

Alfred Cookman (1828–71)

"I am sweeping through the gates, washed in the blood of the Lamb."

Christopher Columbus (1435–1506)

"Father, into thy hands I commend my spirit."

Jonathan Edwards (1703–57)

"Trust in God and you need not fear."

John Eliot (1604–90)

"O come in glory! I have long waited for Thy coming. Let no dark cloud rest on the work of the Indians. Let it live when I am dead. Welcome joy!"

Matthew Henry (1662–1714)

"A life spent in the service of God and communion with Him is the most comfortable and pleasant life that one can live in this present world."

Samuel Hopkins (1721–1803)

"My anchor is well cast, and my ship, though weather-beaten, will outride the storm."

John Knox (1505–72)

"Live in Christ, live in Christ, and the flesh need not fear death."

Cotton Mather (1633–1728)

"I am going where all tears shall be wiped away from my eyes."

Dwight Moody (1837–99)

"I see earth receding; Heaven is opening; God is calling me."

John Newton (1725–1807)

"I am satisfied with the Lord's will."

Thomas Rutherford (1712–71)

"He has indeed been a precious Christ to me, and now I feel him to be my rock, my strength, my rest, my hope, my joy, my all in all."

Sir Walter Scott (1771–1832)

"There is but one Book; bring me the Bible. God bless you all."

Isaac Watts (1674–1748)

"It is a great mercy to me that I have no manner of fear or dread of death."

John Wesley (1703–91)

"The best of all, God is with us."

William Wilberforce (1759–1833)

"I now feel so weaned from earth, my affections so much in Heaven, that I can leave you all without regret, yet I do not love you less, but God more."

Nicolaus Ludwig Zinzendorf (1700–1760)

"Now, my dear son, I am going to the Savior. I am ready; I am quite resigned to the will of my Lord. If he is no longer willing to make use of me here, I am quite ready to go to Him, for there is nothing more in my way."

For additional last words, see Edgar James Meacham, *Manual for Funeral Occasions* (Cincinnati: Standard Publishing Company, 1911).

23

Creating a Eulogy or Remembrance

Funerals in some traditions commonly include a eulogy or remembrance that is written and delivered either by the minister or by a relative or friend of the deceased. Unlike an obituary, which only includes biographical information, a eulogy is an opportunity in more detailed fashion to acknowledge the importance of the life of the person and to remind the survivors of the memories and legacy of the departed. It's often the most personal and unique part of the funeral service. No set or prepackaged template can be used for all eulogies. Sometimes the person the family requests to give the eulogy might ask the minister for suggestions on how to go about writing a eulogy that gives tribute to the deceased and yet brings glory to God.

Some ministers prefer to weave personal comments about the deceased into their meditation or sermon, thus making a separate eulogy unnecessary.

In some services an open time for personal comments and reflections is provided to enable anyone who desires to come to the microphone and voice brief thankfulness to God for the life of the person now deceased. Stories, shared experiences, and humor, when appropriate, may be shared briefly.

How Does One Prepare to Write a Eulogy?

Think through the following and write out some notes that become potential content to use in the eulogy:

How did you and the deceased come to know one another?

What did you and other people appreciate and admire about the deceased?

What will you and others miss most about this person?

Is there a moving or humorous story that captures the essence of this person?

What are some of your favorite memories of this person?

Are there things that stand out about your loved one's personal walk with Christ?

If you could tell the deceased one last thing, what might that be?

What key influences did the deceased have on you or others?

What key words best describe your friend or family member who has died?

Is there a unifying theme that emerges from these thoughts?

What Elements Should Be Considered for Inclusion in a Eulogy?

A brief introduction of yourself and your relation to the deceased.

Family information such as the name of the husband or wife, children, grandchildren, and great-grandchildren, as well as any surviving parents and siblings.

Reference to the person's career and military service, if any.

Reference to the person's schooling.

The person's conversion, church membership, and service.

The deceased's interests, hobbies, and community service.

If available, reference to the individual's favorite hymns, songs, or Scriptures that might be woven into the comments.

Significant stories and memories.

What Elements Should Be Avoided in a Eulogy?

Using a eulogy as an opportunity to get even or expose family secrets.

Using a eulogy to make political statements.

Using a eulogy to question the person's character or spiritual experience.

Using a eulogy to share questionable and inappropriate jokes or humor.

Using unfamiliar vocabulary and undefined, specialized theological terms.

General Suggestions for Eulogies

Generally, a eulogy should not be extemporaneous but something that is thought through, outlined, and written out in advance.

Avoid making this a man- or woman-centered monologue but look for ways to celebrate the grace of Christ at work in the life of the deceased. Look for ways to bring glory to God in the comments made. Recall the words of the apostle Paul, "But by the grace of God I am what I am, and his grace to me was not without effect" (1 Cor. 15:10).

Some ministers like to provide the family with a written copy of the eulogy after the service.

The main prepared eulogy generally runs from three to eight minutes, depending on local customs and circumstances. If it is too short, a wonderful opportunity to give tribute that's deserved is missed. But excessive length risks losing the attention of the congregation and detracting from a God-centered focus.

Use normal conversational vocabulary.

Sometimes the minister will read the obituary notice prior to giving the eulogy or remembrance.

24

Template for a Funeral or Memorial Service

Places, Dates, and Times

Name: _____

Date of the funeral: _____

Time: _____

Location of the funeral:

_____

Location of visitation:

_____

Time of visitation: _____

Time family should arrive for visitation: _____

Time family should arrive for funeral: _____

(*Or* Funeral director will pick family up at:)_____

Burial immediately follows funeral or later? _____

Funeral meal served at _____

_____

Takes place after funeral or after burial? _____

_____

Prayer of Invocation

This is a brief prayer, asking God for comfort at this time of loss and thanking him for the hope of eternal life.

Words of Welcome

Express gratitude on behalf of the family for the presence of the mourners.

Scripture Reading from Old Testament

See suggested readings in chapter 20.

Scripture Reading from New Testament

See suggested readings in chapter 20.

Prayer

Obituary and/or Eulogy or Remembrance

See suggestions in chapter 23. May be given by the pastor or an opportunity may be provided for family and/or friends to speak briefly.

Music

Some funerals include a solo by someone from the congregation or a loved one of the deceased. Often the deceased will have requested that a particular song be sung at the funeral.

Many funerals also include a time of congregational singing and worship. If that is desired, who will lead the worship? What songs will be sung? What instrumentalists are needed?

Meditation

See appendix A.

Prayer and/or Song

Military Participation?

If the deceased was a veteran, there may be a military honor guard on hand to provide an expression of gratitude for the person's life and service.

Graveside Committal Service

See suggestions in part 3.

Scripture

Prayer

Words of Committal

Benediction

Military Honors?

If a military honor guard is present, it is customary for this unit to remove the flag from the casket, fold it, and present it to a member of the family.

Appendixes

Appendix A

Funeral Message Preparation

Principles for Funeral Messages

1. Minister the comfort of the gospel hope to family and friends. Do not berate or lecture.

2. Avoid lengthy sermons. Be brief. This is a stressful time for those who are grieving. More than five to ten minutes for the sermon itself indicates insensitivity in the preacher unless the family requests a longer, traditional sermon. In some settings the stature of the deceased and/or particularly tragic circumstances may also require a more lengthy address. Messages typically are a logical development of a basic idea (or two) in a text, not verse-by-verse expositions—few, if any, will have their Bibles with them to follow along.

3. It is God who should be worshiped and praised, rather than the human accomplishments of the deceased. Acknowledge God's grace more than laud human accomplishment. Although it is certainly appropriate to give thanks for the good God has worked through this

individual's life, care must be taken not to imply that divine acceptance is based on human goodness—the message the world almost inevitably hears.

4. Hold the cross high. This is not an evangelistic sermon. Most pastors, however, will address more nonbelievers at funerals and weddings than at any other time. The truths of the gospel need to be plainly stated because they bear upon every person's ultimate condition.

5. If the deceased was not known as a professing believer, do not pass judgment on his/her spiritual condition. Neither should the pastor raise false hopes by assuring the family that their departed loved one is with the Lord. State the blessings of the gospel that those who profess Jesus Christ share without saying such apply to this person. Preachers in past generations said that when preaching a funeral for one who was not known as a believer they would "read the man's facts, then preach the Lord's gospel"; that is, let people know whose funeral it is by some personal reference, but then move on to preach the gospel without judging whether the one applied to the other. This is still good advice.

6. Simple truths sincerely spoken are required. This is not the time for theological treatises or exegetical insights. The simple truths of our resurrection and reunion based upon God's grace are the most compelling, meaningful, and comforting things you can say. The gospel has real power in these moments. Do not be afraid to let the Word do its work.

Content of Funeral Messages

Key concept: begin personally, then move higher.

1. Begin with something personal related to the deceased or his/her family. Let the family know you care for them and their loved one. Address the family directly and let others listen in by projecting so all can hear.

2. Tie the personal reference to a gospel text evident in the text(s) you read prior to the message.

3. Logically develop the hope Christians have in the face of death based on the theme you have introduced and the passage(s) you have read. Funeral messages typically contain references to the joys of heaven, the believer's release from suffering, the ultimate reunion with loved ones, and so on. All funeral sermons must include explanations of Christ's victory over sin and death, believers' resurrection hope, and the need of all the living to claim this gospel by faith alone.

4. Make sure all know that this person's hope is in Christ's work, not the person's work.

5. Genuinely rejoice in the joy deceased believers now know, but at the same time affirm the right for loved ones to grieve for the separation they now experience.

6. End with hope, the assurance of Christ's victory.

Cautions for Funeral Messages

1. Be cautious about references such as "We are gathering here to *celebrate* the passing of _____ into glory." Yes, there are truths in which believers can rejoice, but there is much pain present too. Jesus wept in the face of death. We should not treat the horror of a fallen

world's ultimate consequence without hope or without regard for the real pain it causes. Do not forbid grief.

2. Provide the comfort of your sympathy to the families of those that were not known as believers. If you do not know what else to say, you can at least say that you are sorry for the family's loss and that you grieve for their hurt. Your sorrow is no more an endorsement of faithlessness than your callousness would be an affirmation of the gospel. Remember, ultimately you do not know others' hearts. If you have questions about the spiritual state of the deceased, simply preach the gospel treasures of those who *do* have faith without saying this person does, or does not, share in them.

3. Avoid exaggeration of anyone's good life. But at a believer's funeral certainly let the glory of the deceased's life and hope in Jesus fill your message. It is not at all inappropriate to cite the goodness that God has accomplished through a believer's life or to rejoice in the service and testimony such a person has provided the kingdom.

4. Do not use the funeral as a time to guilt-trip friends and relatives into heaven. Although it is certainly legitimate to invite others to share the gospel hope, and even to express the concern the deceased may have had for others' salvation, these appeals should be made with compassion, not futile, manipulative condemnation.

5. Remember, your *primary* task is to comfort, not to evangelize. Even though evangelistic truths are presented, this is a funeral sermon. The *main* purpose is to bring the hope of the gospel to loved ones facing the pain of death.

Adapted from Bryan Chapell, *Christ-Centered Preaching* (Grand Rapids: Baker Books, 1994), 344–46. Used by permission.

Appendix B

Funeral Planning Guide

Full name of deceased	
Date of service	
Time of service	
Location of service	
Mortician	
• Name	
• Address	
• Phone	
• Email	
Viewing/Visitation	
• Date(s)	
• Time(s)	
• Location	

Dates concerning deceased (birth, death, and age)	
Contact person	
• Name	
• Phone	
• Email	
Surviving relatives	
• Husband or wife	
• Children	
• Parents	
• Brothers/sisters	
• Grandchildren	
• Other relatives	
Memorial fund and recipients	
Life and eulogy information (education, jobs, offices held, notable accomplishments, honors received, etc.)	
Participants in funeral	
Cremation arrangements?	
Casket at funeral? Open or closed?	
Pallbearers	

Musicians (names and contact information)	
• Organist/pianist	
• Vocalists and selections	
Hymns	
Scripture readings	
• Old Testament	
• New Testament	
Special requests	
Meditation	
• Title	
• Text	
Bulletin cover selected? How many?	
Sound technician contact information	
Burial	
• Time	
• Place	
• Special arrangements	
Family funeral lunch/dinner?	
Other	

Appendix C

Pastor's Funeral Record

Name and age of deceased	Date and place of death	Date and place of funeral

Burial location	Funeral message	Follow-up actions

Appendix D

Preplanning Funeral Form

Funeral and Burial Instructions

I, _____, on _____ (date) herewith indicate the following instructions concerning my funeral/memorial service:

1. Service to be held at

_____

_____

_____

_____

_____

2. Service to be led by

_____

_____

_____

_____

_____

3. I wish to use the following funeral director

   Name _____

   Address _____

   Phone _____

   Email _____

4. Burial arrangements

   Cemetery/memorial gardens

   _____

   Are facilities prearranged?

   Lot number _____

   Block or section _____

Grave number _____

Cremation? _____

5. Preferences for funeral/memorial service (music, Scripture, etc.)

_____

_____

_____

_____

_____

6. Preferences

Casket _____

Vault _____

Vital Statistics

Full name _____

Address _____

Phone _____

Email _____

Single _____ Married _____ Widowed _____ Divorced _____

Name of husband/wife _____

Date of birth _____

Place of birth _____

Occupation _____

Name of father _____

Name of mother _____

Schools attended

_____

_____

_____

_____

If veteran, war and rank _____

Organizations and offices held

_____

_____

_____

_____

Church membership _____

Living children

Name	Address	Phone	Email

Living brothers and sisters

Name	Address	Phone	Email

Living grandchildren/great-grandchildren

Name	Address	Phone	Email

Paul E. Engle is an ordained minister who has served in pastoral ministry in churches in Pennsylvania, Connecticut, Illinois, and Michigan. Dr. Engle has also taught as a visiting instructor in the Doctor of Ministry and practical theology departments of Trinity Evangelical Divinity School, New Geneva Theological Seminary, Knox Theological Seminary, Reformed Theological Seminary, and Dallas Theological Seminary. He also teaches church leaders in the Philippines, Romania, Uganda, Cuba, and East Asia. He earned degrees from Houghton College, Wheaton College Graduate School, and Westminster Theological Seminary. He is the author of eight books, including *The Baker Wedding Handbook*.